Mathcounts National Competition
Team Round Solutions

1990 – 2000

Jane Chen

http://www.mymathcounts.com/index.php

This is a solution book for 1990 - 2000 Mathcounts National Competition Team Round problems. Please contact mymathcounts@gmail.com for suggestions, corrections, or clarifications of the solutions.

Contributors

Jane Chen, Author.
Yongcheng Chen, Ph.D., Reviewer

© 2017 mymathcounts.com. All rights reserved. Printed in the United States of America

ISBN-13: 978-1543272307
ISBN-10: 1543272304

Table of Contents

This page is intentionally left blank.

1990 Mathcounts National Team Round Solutions

1. **Solution:** 55.
Method 1:
There are $5 \times 5 = 25$ 1 by 1 squares.

There are $4 \times 4 = 16$ 2 by 2 squares.

There are $3 \times 3 = 9$ 3 by 3 squares.

There are $2 \times 2 = 4$ 4 by 4 squares.

There is 1 5 by 5 squares.
In total, there are $25 + 16 + 9 + 4 + 1 = 55$ squares.

Method 2:

The total number of squares, N, is

$N = n^2 + (n-1)^2 + (n-2)^2 + \ldots + 1^2$ where n is the number of rows (or columns).

It follows that $N = 5^2 + 4^2 + 3^2 + 2^2 + 1^2 = 55$.

2. **Solution:** 7.

The sum of the two-digit numbers formed by the four pairs of preceding digits of 83 46 38 97 5 and 79 86 95 64 2 is $83 + 46 + 38 + 97 = 264$ and $79 + 86 + 95 + 64 = 326$.

We are given that the last digit of each card number is the integer remainder when the sum is divided by x.

It follows that

$$264 - 5 \equiv 0 \bmod x$$
$$326 - 2 \equiv 0 \bmod x$$

Simplifying, we have

$$259 \equiv 0 \bmod x$$
$$324 \equiv 0 \bmod x$$

The greatest common factor of 259 and 324 is 7, so $x = 7$.

3. **Solution:** $\dfrac{1}{3}$.

From the digits 3, 4, 5, 6, 8, and 10, we can create two right triangles: (3, 4, 5), and (6, 8, 10).

For a triangle with sides (3, 4, 5), there are $\binom{3}{2} = 3$ ways to choose 2 sides from

3. Multiplying by 2 to account for the order of the dice, (ie. Die 1 shows 3, Die 2 shows 4; Die 1 shows 4, Die 2 shows 3), we get $3 \times 2 = 6$ ways.

2

For a triangle with sides (6, 8, 10), there are $\binom{3}{2} = 3$ ways to choose 2 sides from 3. Multiplying by 2 to account for the order of the dice, (i.e. Die 1 shows 6, Die 2 shows 8; Die 1 shows 8, Die 2 shows 6), we get $3 \times 2 = 6$ ways.

So the number of ways to roll two six-sided dice such that the two faces showing have numbers that could correspond to any two sides of a right triangle is $(3 + 3) \times 2$. There are $6 \times 6 = 36$ total combinations when rolling two six-sided dice.

The desired solution is then $P = \dfrac{(3+3) \times 2}{6 \times 6} = \dfrac{1}{3}$.

4. **Solution:** $63\sqrt{3} + 63$.

The perimeter of the polygon is:

$$32\sqrt{3} + \sqrt{32^2 - 16^2} + \sqrt{16^2 - 8^2} + \sqrt{8^2 - 4^2}$$

$$+ \sqrt{4^2 - 2^2} + \sqrt{2^2 - 1^2} + \sqrt{(32\sqrt{3})^2 + 32^2 - 1}$$

$$= 32\sqrt{3} + 16\sqrt{3} + 8\sqrt{3} + 2\sqrt{3} + \sqrt{3}$$

$$= 63\sqrt{3} + 63$$

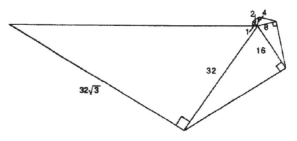

5. **Solution:** 71.

The LCM of 5, 3, and 7 is equivalent to their identical score.

LCM (5, 3, 7) = 105.

So Adam played 105/5 games, his younger brother played 105/7 games, and the computer played 105/3 games.

The fewest number of games they could have played in order for this tie to be possible is 105/5 + 105/3 + 105/7 = 71.

6. **Solution:** $w = 2z$.
We use letters to represent the symbols. Let x represent the square, y represent the triangle, z represent the circle, and w represent the shaded ellipse.
We have:

fig. 1

$2x + y = 8z$ (1)
$x = y + z$ (2)
$z + w = x$ (3)

fig. 2

From (2), we have $y = x - z$. Substituting in $x - z$ for y into (1), we get

$2x + (x - z) = 8z$

$\Rightarrow 3x = 9z$

$\Rightarrow x = 3z$

fig. 3

Substituting in $3z$ for x into (3), we get
$z + w = 3z$.

Solving for w in terms of z, we get $w = 2z$. Thus, the shaded ellipses is equal to 2 circles.

7. **Solution:** 7.
There are $9 - 1 + 1 = 9$ one-digit numbers, $99 - 10 + 1 = 90$ two-digit numbers, and $999 - 100 + 1 = 900$ three-digit numbers. Let there be x four-digit numbers until the 3001st digit is written.

$1 \times 9 + 2 \times 90 + 3 \times 900 + 4 \times x = 3001$ $\Rightarrow$ $x = 128$.

Writing 128 numbers from 1000, we end the number 1127. The 3001st digit is then 7.

8. **Solution:** 20 cents.
Two hundred tickets sold for a dollar each makes 200 dollars. The sum of the total amount of the three prizes is $10 + 50 + 100 = 160$. The lottery commission makes

$200 - 160 = 40$ dollars. Since there are 200 tickets, it makes
$$\frac{200 \times 1 - 10 - 50 - 100}{200} = \$0.2 = 20 \text{ cents per ticket.}$$

9. **Solution:** 6 seconds.
Substituting in 128 for v_0, 144 for s_0, and 336 for s into the formula, we get
$336 = -16t^2 + 128t + 144$.

Solving the quadratic equation for t for the positive solution, we get $t = 6$ seconds.

10. **Solution:** $4x^2 + 4xy$.
Since the volume of the box is xyz, we can assume that the dimension of box is x by y by z.

The surface area of the box is $2(xy + yz + zx)$. The surface area of the initial rectangular piece of paper before it was cut is $(z + 2x)(2y + 2x)$.

It follows that the total area of the paper that was thrown away is the difference between the surface area of the initial piece of paper and the surface area of the box, or $(z + 2x)(2y + 2x) - 2(xy + yz + zx) = 4x^2 + 4xy$.

1991 Mathcounts National Team Round Solutions

1. **Solution:** 198.
The surface area of one cube with side 2 is $2 \times 2 \times 6 = 24$ and so the total surface area of eight cubes with side 2 is $24 \times 8 = 192$.

The surface area of one cube of side 3 is $3 \times 3 \times 6 = 54$.

The total sum of the surface area of eight 2 by 2 by 2 cubes and one 1 by 1 by 1 cube is $192 + 54$. However, we need to subtract the surface area that is blocked because of the corner insertions.

The surface area that is blocked by the cube of side 1 when the cube of side 2 inches is inserted in a corner is $1 \times 1 \times 3 = 3$. Since there are eight 2 by 2 by 2 cubes, the total surface area that is blocked is $3 \times 8 = 24$. We must subtract 24 two times, once from our calculation of the surface area of the eight 2 by 2 by 2 cubes, and another time from our calculation of the surface area of the 1 by 1 by 1 cube.

The desired solution is then $192 + 54 - 24 - 24 = 198$.

2. **Solution:** $36 - 4\pi - 12\sqrt{3}$.
Since $AC = 3$ and $AB = 2\sqrt{3}$, looking at right triangle ABC, we have $BC = \sqrt{3}$ and $\angle BAC = 30°$.

The area of $\triangle ABC = \dfrac{1}{2} \times 3 \times \sqrt{3}$.

The area of sector ABD is $\dfrac{\pi(2\sqrt{3})^2}{360} \times 30 = \pi$.

The area b is equal to twice the difference of area of $\triangle ABC$ and sector ABD, or

$b = 2(\pi - \dfrac{3\sqrt{3}}{2}) = 2\pi - 3\sqrt{3}$.

The area of a is equal to the area of twice b subtracted from the area of the quarter-circle with radius $AB = 2\sqrt{3}$, or

$$a = \frac{1}{4}\pi(2\sqrt{3})^2 - 2b = 3\pi - 2(2\pi - 3\sqrt{3}) = -\pi + 6\sqrt{3}.$$

The shaded area equals the area of the square minus 4 times the area of a and b, or

$$6 \times 6 - 4(a + b) = 36 - 4(\pi + 3\sqrt{3}) = 36 - 4\pi - 12\sqrt{3}.$$

3. **Solution:** 4: 20.

At 4 o'clock, the minute hand and the hour hand form an angle of 120°.

In 60 minutes, the minute hand moves 360°. So the minute hand moves at a rate of 6° per minute.

In 60 minutes, the hour hand moves 30°. So the hour hand moves at a rate of $1/2°$ per minute.

This means that the minute hand moves at a relative speed of $\frac{11°}{2}$ per minute.

In order for the minute hand and the hour hand to be exactly 10° apart, the minute hand needs to move an angle of 110° at the relative speed of $\frac{11°}{2}$ per minute in t minutes.

In order to find t, we have:

$$t \times \frac{11°}{2} = 110° \Rightarrow t = 110 \times \frac{2}{11} = 20 \text{ minutes.}$$

The time will be 4:20.

4. Solution: 3.
Since the volume of the hemisphere is equal to the volume of the original bubble, we have

$$\frac{4}{3}\pi\left(3\sqrt[3]{2}\right)^3 \times \frac{1}{2} = \frac{4}{3}\pi\, r^3 \qquad\qquad \Rightarrow \qquad r = 3.$$

5. Solution: 43.
There are $\left\lfloor\dfrac{100}{3}\right\rfloor - \left\lfloor\dfrac{100}{12}\right\rfloor = 25$ numbers that are multiples of 3 but not multiples of 4. The student correctly answered these 25 questions.

There are $\left\lfloor\dfrac{100}{4}\right\rfloor - \left\lfloor\dfrac{100}{12}\right\rfloor = 17$ numbers that are multiples of 4 but not multiples of 3. The student correctly answered these 3 questions.

The total number of questions the student got correct by marking every item that is a multiple of 3 false and all others true is $25 + 17 = 43$.

Note: The student incorrectly answered the questions that are multiples of 3 and 4:
$$\left\lfloor\frac{100}{12}\right\rfloor = 8.$$

The student incorrectly answered the questions that are neither multiple of 3 nor 4:
$$100 - \left(\left\lfloor\frac{100}{3}\right\rfloor + \left\lfloor\frac{100}{4}\right\rfloor - \left\lfloor\frac{100}{12}\right\rfloor\right) = 50$$

6. Solution: $11\dfrac{1}{4}$.
Since $AD = 12$ and $CD = 9$, looking at right triangle ACD, we have $AC = 15$.

Since $\triangle AGE \sim \triangle ADC$, we have

$$\frac{AG}{EG} = \frac{AD}{CD}$$

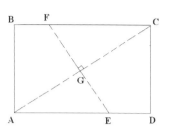

$$\Rightarrow \quad \frac{\dfrac{15}{2}}{\dfrac{EF}{2}} = \frac{12}{9}$$

$$\Rightarrow \quad EF = 11\frac{1}{4}.$$

7. Solution: 1/19.
Suppose Curtis is already in a group. There are 19 students and one spot left, so
Cameron's chance of being in the same group as Curtis is 1/19. The desired
solution is 1/19.

8. Solution: 95.
We follow the pattern and add the next figure:

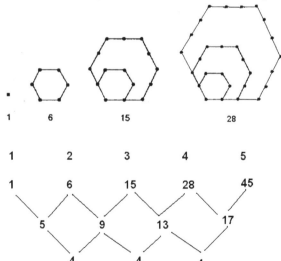

The sum is 95.

Note: Hexagonal Numbers: N = $\dfrac{n(4n-2)}{2}$, where n is an integer.

9. Solution: 30 cm^2.

Method 1.
The area of triangle ADE is

$$S_{\triangle ADE} = \frac{(3+9)\times 9}{2} = 54.$$

Triangle CEF is similar to triangle ADE.

The area of triangle CEF can be obtained as following:

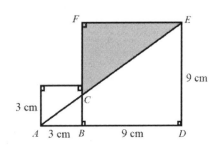

$$\frac{S_{\triangle CEF}}{S_{\triangle ADE}} = \left(\frac{9}{12}\right)^2 = \left(\frac{3}{4}\right)^2 = \frac{9}{16}$$

$$\Rightarrow \quad S_{\triangle CEF} = \frac{9}{16}S_{\triangle ADE} = \frac{9}{16}\times 54 = \frac{243}{8} = 30.375 \approx 30.$$

Method 2.
Triangle CEF is similar to triangle ADE.

It follows that

$$\frac{ED}{CB} = \frac{AD}{AB} \quad \Rightarrow \quad CB = \frac{AB \times ED}{AD} = \frac{3\times 9}{12} = \frac{9}{4}$$

$$S_{\triangle CEF} = \frac{FE \times FC}{2} = \frac{9\times(9-\frac{9}{4})}{2} = \frac{243}{8} \approx 30.$$

10. **Solution:** 198.
Let m be the number of minutes that the video can be recorded on long play for one minute on short play.

$$\frac{120}{360} = \frac{1}{m} \qquad \Rightarrow \qquad m = 3$$

Let n be the number of minutes that the video can be recorded on extra-long play for one minute on long play.

$$\frac{240}{360} = \frac{1}{n} \qquad \Rightarrow \qquad n = 1.5$$

32 minutes on short play will be $32 \times 3 = 96$ minutes in extra-long play.

44 minutes on long play will be 44 × 1.5 = 66 minutes in extra-long play. Since we are given that the number of minutes that the video can be recorded on extra-long play is 60 × 6 = 360, the remaining number of minutes left for extra-long play is 360− 96 − 66 = 198.

1992 Mathcounts National Ream Solutions

1. **Solution:** 17 times.

We know that $\dfrac{10}{7} = 1 + 0.\overline{428571}$

The decimal digits repeat every 6 digits.

Power of 10:	10^1	10^2	10^3	10^4	10^5	10^6
Integer part of the quotient:	1	14	142	1428	14285	142857

$100 \equiv 16 \times 6 + 4 \qquad (\bmod\ 6)$

The last four digits of the quotient will be 1428, which includes one "4".

So the digit "4" appears $(16 + 1) = 17$ times.

2. **Solution:** 04.

Method 1:

Since 2 and 100 are not relatively prime, we can't directly apply any theorems.

Note $2^{12} \equiv -4 \ (\bmod\ 100)$

$$2^{222} \equiv (2^{12})^{18} \times 2^6$$
$$\equiv (-2^2)^{18} \times 2^6$$
$$\equiv 2^{36} \times 2^6$$
$$\equiv (2^{12})^3 \times 2^6$$
$$\equiv (-2^2)^3 \times 2^6$$
$$\equiv -2^{12}$$
$$\equiv -(-2^2)$$
$$\equiv 4 \qquad \bmod\ 100$$

The last two digits are 04.

Method 2:

$$2^{222} \equiv R \quad \mod 100$$
$$2^{222} \equiv R_1 \quad \mod 25 \tag{1}$$
$$2^{222} \equiv R_2 \quad \mod 4 \tag{2}$$

We know that $\phi(25) = 20$

(1) $\quad\Rightarrow\quad 2^2 \equiv R_1 \quad \mod 25 \quad\Rightarrow\quad R_1 \equiv 4 \quad \mod 25$

(2) $\quad\Rightarrow\quad (2^2)^{111} \equiv R_2 \quad \mod 4 \quad\Rightarrow\quad R_2 \equiv 0 \quad \mod 4$

The first term common to both (1) and (2) is 04.

3. Solution: 7.
With the use of a calculator, we can get the smallest n to be 7.
$$\frac{1}{1} + \frac{1}{4} + \frac{1}{9} + \frac{1}{16} + \frac{1}{25} + \frac{1}{36} + \frac{1}{49} = 1.51179052 > 1.5$$

4. Solution: 20.
As shown in the figure below, one third of the shaded area equals the area of the sector OAB minus the area of $\triangle$OAB, or
$$2(\frac{\pi \times 6^2}{6} - \frac{\sqrt{3}}{4} \times 6^2).$$

The total shaded area is: $3 \times 2(\dfrac{\pi \times 6^2}{6} - \dfrac{\sqrt{3}}{4} \times 6^2) = 20$.

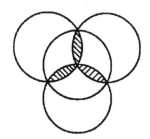

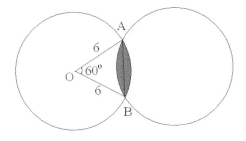

5. Solution: 13.
By Heron's Theorem, the area of triangle, A, can be calculated as:

13

$$A = \sqrt{s(s-a)(s-b)(s-c)} = r \times s$$

where $s = \frac{1}{2}(a+b+c)$.

$$s = \frac{1}{2}(14+6+x+8+x) = 14+x.$$

$$\sqrt{(14+x)(14+x-14)(14+x-6-x)(14+x-8-x)} = 4(14+x)$$

$$\Rightarrow \sqrt{(14+x)x \times 8 \times 6} = 4(14+x)$$

$$\Rightarrow \quad 4\sqrt{3x(14+x)} = 4(14+x)$$

$$\Rightarrow \quad \sqrt{3x(14+x)} = 14+x$$

$$\Rightarrow \quad \sqrt{3x} = \sqrt{14+x} \quad \Rightarrow \quad x = 7$$

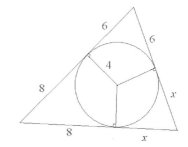

The length of the shortest side of the triangle is $7 + 6 = 13$.

6. **Solution:** 206 pages.

Pages 1 through 9 use	1×9	$= 9$	digits	9 pages
Pages 10 through 99 use	2×90	$= 180$	digits	90 pages
Pages 100 through X use	$3 \times x$	$= 3x$	digits	x pages

Since 510 digits were printed, it follows that
$3x = 510 - (180 + 9)$.

Solving for x, we get $x = 107$.

The book has $107 + 90 + 9 = 206$ pages.

7. **Solution:** 37.

$$\frac{(17+50)\times 80}{2} + \frac{50y}{2} = \frac{1}{5} \times 100 \times 100$$

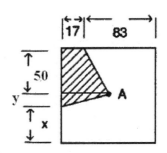

Solving for y, we get $y = 13$.
It follows that $x = 50 - 13 = 37$.

8. **Solution:** 7.5.

As shown in the figure, the region is a rectangle.

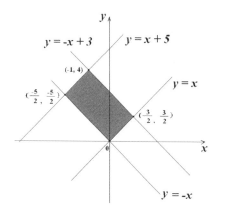

The width of the rectangle is:

$$\sqrt{(\frac{3}{2})^2 + (\frac{3}{2})^2} = \frac{3}{\sqrt{2}}$$

The length of the rectangle is:

$$\sqrt{(-\frac{5}{2})^2 + (-\frac{5}{2})^2} = \frac{5}{\sqrt{2}}$$

The area is then: $\dfrac{3}{\sqrt{2}} \times \dfrac{5}{\sqrt{2}} = \dfrac{15}{2} = 7.5$.

9. **Solution:** 9.

First we draw two cards from each suit, which will be $4 \times 2 = 8$ cards. If we draw one card more card, regardless what suit this card is, we are guaranteed to have three cards from the same suit. So the number of cards that must be selected is 9.

10. **Solution:** $\dfrac{2}{5}$.

The digital root of a number is also the result of taking mod 9 on the number.

$1^3 \equiv 1$ mod 9
$2^3 \equiv 8$ mod 9
$3^3 \equiv 0$ mod 9
$4^3 \equiv 1$ mod 9
$5^3 \equiv 8$ mod 9
$6^3 \equiv (-3)^3 = 0$ mod 9
$7^3 \equiv (-2)^3 = 1$ mod 9
$8^3 \equiv (-1)^3 = 8$ mod 9
$9^3 \equiv 0$ mod 9
$10^3 \equiv 1$ mod 9

The probability is $P = \dfrac{4}{10} = \dfrac{2}{5}$.

1993 Mathcounts National Team Round Solutions

1. Solution: 54.

$$(78900000345)^2 = (789 \times 10^5 + 345)^2 = 789^2 \times 10^{10} + 345^2 + 2 \times 789 \times 10^5 \times 345$$

345^2 is 6 digits and $2 \times 789 \times 345$ end in a 0, so none of the digits will overlap with each other. Since we are only interested in calculating the sum of the digits, we can ignore all zeros and simplify the expression into:

$$789^2 + 345^2 + 2 \times 789 \times 345 = 622521 + 119025 + 544410$$

The sum of the digits is $6 + 2 + 2 + 5 + 2 + 1 + 1 + 1 + 9 + 0 + 2 + 5 + 5 + 4 + 4 + 4 + 1 + 0 = 54$.

2. Solution: -3.

Let two numbers be a and b. We know that $a + b = 12$ and $ab = -4$.

So the sum of their reciprocals is $\dfrac{1}{a} + \dfrac{1}{b} = \dfrac{a+b}{ab} = \dfrac{12}{-4} = -3$.

3. Solution: 875

C can be 1, 5, or 6. Since the hundreds digit of the result is a different digit D, C can not be 1.

$$\begin{array}{r} ABC \\ \times\ \ C \\ \hline DBC \end{array}$$

Regardless of whether C is 5 or 6, A can only be 1, otherwise the product would be a four-digit number.

If $C = 5$, we have:
$$\begin{array}{r} 1B5 \\ \times\ \ 5 \\ \hline DB5 \end{array}$$

To achieve the largest value for D, we need to maximize the value of B. The largest possible value for B is 5, resulting in a product of 875.

If $C = 6$, we have
$$\begin{array}{r} 1B6 \\ \times\ \ 6 \\ \hline DB6 \end{array}$$
. This case yields no results.

4. Solution: 42.

16

In order to achieve a sum of 14 between three numbers, the parity of the numbers can be the two following ways
1. Even, Even, Even
2. Odd, Odd, Even.

Since Anna says, "I know that Brett and Chris have different numbers," her number must be odd. Otherwise if her number were even, then the other two numbers could be equal to each other. For example, if her number was 2, then the other two numbers could be 6 and 6, and she would not be able to say that Brett and Chris have different numbers.

This rules out the first case, and tells us that the three numbers must be odd, odd, and even. Since Brett is able to tell that all three numbers were different but he is not able to know their values, Brett's number must also be odd but not 1, 3, nor 5.

Otherwise, if his number were 1, 3, or 5, it would match with Anna's number.

This leaves 7, 9, or 11 for Brett.

If his number were 11, he would know all three numbers, since $14 = 11 + 1 + 2$, and Anna's number must be 1, 3 or 5.

If Brett's number were 9, we would have $14 - 9 = 5$ as the sum of the other two numbers. 5 can be written as either $1 + 4$ or $3 + 2$, so Brett would not be able to know each person's numbers.

If Brett's number were 7, we have $14 - 7 = 7$ as the sum of the other two numbers. 7 can be written as either $5 + 2$ or $3 + 4$ or $1 + 6$, so Brett would not be able to know each person's numbers.

At this point, we have determined that Brett's number can be either 9 or 7.

We also know that Chris was able to determine the three numbers. His number could be 6, 4, or 2.

If his number were 2, he would not be able to determine each person's numbers since 14 can be written as either $5 + 7 + 2$ or $3 + 9 + 2$.

If his number were 4, he would not be able to determine each person's numbers since 14 can be written as 14 or 3 + 7 + 4 or 1 + 9 + 4.

If his number were 6, he would be able to determine each person's numbers since 14 can only be written as 1 + 7 + 6.

And so, the product is $1 \times 7 \times 6 = 42$.

5. **Solution:** 84th position.
When the first letter is C, we have $4! = 24$ strings:
$\underline{C} \underline{} \underline{} \underline{} \underline{}$

When the first letter is N, we have $4! = 24$ strings:
$\underline{N} \underline{} \underline{} \underline{} \underline{}$

When the first letter is O, we have $4! = 24$ strings:
$\underline{O} \underline{} \underline{} \underline{} \underline{}$

When the first two letters are TC, we have $3! = 6$ strings:
$\underline{T} \underline{C} \underline{} \underline{} \underline{}$

When the first three letters are TNC, we have $2! = 2$ strings:
$\underline{T} \underline{N} \underline{C} \underline{} \underline{}$

When the first three letters are TNO, we have $2! = 2$ strings:
$\underline{T} \underline{N} \underline{O} \underline{} \underline{}$

The next term that follows is:
$\underline{T} \underline{N} \underline{U} \underline{C} \underline{O}$
$24 + 24 + 24 + 6 + 2 + 2 + 1 = 83$

The next term will be what we want:
$\underline{T} \underline{N} \underline{U} \underline{O} \underline{C}$

This term is in 84th position.

6. **Solution:** 4.34.

The shaded area is equal to the difference between the area of the square $ABCD$ and $2(a + b) + b$, or

$$100 - \frac{1}{2}\pi \times 100 + b \ .$$

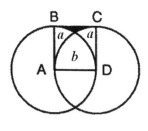

The area of equilateral triangle AED is:

$$y = \frac{\sqrt{3}}{4} \times 10^2 = 25\sqrt{3} \qquad (1)$$

The area of the sector AED is:

$$y + x = \frac{1}{6} \times \pi \times 10^2 = \frac{50\pi}{3}$$

Or $x = \dfrac{50\pi}{3} - 25\sqrt{3} \qquad (2)$

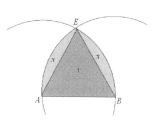

Substituting (1) and (2) into $b = y + 2x$, we get

$$b = \frac{100\pi}{3} - 25\sqrt{3} \ .$$

The desired solution is

$$100 - \frac{1}{2}\pi \times 100 + b = 100 - 50\pi + \frac{100\pi}{3} - 25\sqrt{3} = 4.34$$

7. **Solution:** 302.7.

Let V_1 be the volume of the middle-sized frustum, and V_2 be the volume of the large frustum.

The ratio of the volumes of two frustums can be written as:

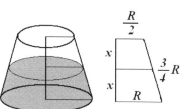

$$\frac{V_1}{V_2} = \frac{\dfrac{1}{3}x[\pi R^2 + \pi(\frac{3}{4}R)^2 + \sqrt{\pi R^2 \times \pi(\frac{3}{4}R)^2}]}{\dfrac{1}{3} \times 2x[\pi R^2 + \pi(\frac{1}{2}R)^2 + \sqrt{\pi R^2 \times \pi(\frac{1}{2}R)^2}]}$$

$$= \frac{200}{V_2} \implies \quad V_2 \approx 302.7.$$

8. Solution: $\dfrac{100}{201}$.

We know that $\dfrac{1}{n(n+k)} = \dfrac{1}{k}(\dfrac{1}{n} - \dfrac{1}{n-k})$, so $\dfrac{1}{1 \times 3} = \dfrac{1}{2}(\dfrac{1}{1} - \dfrac{1}{3})$.

We have

$\dfrac{1}{1 \times 3} + \dfrac{1}{3 \times 5} + \dfrac{1}{5 \times 7} + ... + \dfrac{1}{199 \times 201}$

$= \dfrac{1}{2}(\dfrac{1}{1} - \dfrac{1}{3}) + \dfrac{1}{2}(\dfrac{1}{3} - \dfrac{1}{5}) + \dfrac{1}{2}(\dfrac{1}{5} - \dfrac{1}{7}) + ... + \dfrac{1}{2}(\dfrac{1}{199} - \dfrac{1}{201})$

$= \dfrac{1}{2}(\dfrac{1}{1} - \dfrac{1}{3} + \dfrac{1}{3} - \dfrac{1}{5} + \dfrac{1}{5} - \dfrac{1}{7} + ... + \dfrac{1}{199} - \dfrac{1}{201})$

$= \dfrac{1}{2}(\dfrac{1}{1} - \dfrac{1}{201}) = \dfrac{1}{2} \times \dfrac{200}{201} = \dfrac{100}{201}$.

9. Solution: 5.
The smallest possible value of the sum of three faces is $1 + 2 + 3 = 6$, meaning that the number 5 cannot be a sum.

On a die, we are not able to see 1 and 6 at the same time, as well as 2 and 5, and 3 and 4.

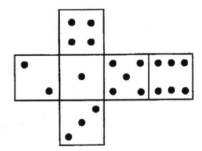

So, these expressions are not possible:
$\underline{1 + 6 + 2 = 9}$, $\underline{1 + 6 + 3 = 10}$,
  $\underline{1 + 6 + 4 = 11}$, $\underline{1 + 6 +}$
$5 = 12$
$\underline{2 + 5 + 1 = 8}$, $\underline{2 + 5 + 3 = 10}$, $\underline{2 + 5 + 4 = 11}$, $\underline{2 + 5 + 6 = 13}$
$\underline{3 + 4 + 1 = 8}$, $\underline{3 + 4 + 2 = 9}$, $\underline{3 + 4 + 5 = 11}$, $\underline{3 + 4 + 6 = 13}$

9 can be written as $2 + 3 + 4$,
10 can be written as $1 + 5 + 4$,
11 can be written as $2 + 3 + 6$, and
12 can be written as $2 + 4 + 6$.

However,
$8 = \underline{2+5}+1 = \underline{3+4}+1$ is not possible and
$13 = 6+\underline{4+3} = 6+\underline{5+2}$ is not possible.

There are three sums that are not possible: 5, 8, and 13.

10. **Solution:** 6.

$$\frac{a+b}{b+c}=\frac{6}{7} \quad \Rightarrow \quad 7a+b=6c \qquad (1)$$

$$\frac{b+c}{c+a}=\frac{7}{8} \quad \Rightarrow \quad 7a=8b+c \qquad (2)$$

Solving (1) and (2) for a and b in terms of c, we get $b=\frac{5}{9}c$ and $a=\frac{7}{9}c$.

$$14=a+b+c=\frac{7}{9}c+\frac{5}{9}c+c=\frac{21}{9}c=\frac{7}{3}c \quad \Rightarrow \quad c=6.$$

1994 National Team Round Solutions:

1. **Solution:** -1.
$$4 \times x - 4 - x = 3x - 4$$
$$2 \times x - 2 - x = x - 2$$

$$(3x - 4)(x - 2) - (3x - 4) - (x - 2) = 31 \qquad \Rightarrow \qquad 3x^2 - 14x - 17 = 0$$

Solving the quadratic, we get $x = -1$ or $x = 17/3$. The integer value is then $x = -1$.

2. **Solution:** $\dfrac{16}{81}$.

Since we only are interested in the ratio of the two areas, we can assume that $AE = 3 \times 3 \times 3 = 27$.

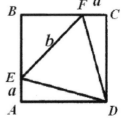

$$AD = \frac{2}{3} AE = \frac{2}{3} \times 27 = 18;$$

$$AC = \frac{2}{3} AD = \frac{2}{3} \times 18 = 12;$$

$$AB = \frac{2}{3} AC = \frac{2}{3} \times 12 = 8.$$

The ratio of the two shaded areas is $\dfrac{AC^2 - AB^2}{AE^2 - AD^2} = \dfrac{12^2 - 8^2}{27^2 - 18^2} = \dfrac{16}{81}$.

3. **Solution:** 2.07.

Let a be the length of one leg of the right triangle and b be the side length of the equilateral triangle. Let S be the area of the equilateral triangle.

We have
$$S_{ABCD} = 2S + a^2$$
$$\Rightarrow \qquad 2S + a^2 = 4$$
$$\Rightarrow \qquad 2 \times \frac{\sqrt{3}}{4} b^2 + b^2 - 2^2 = 4$$

22

$$\Rightarrow \quad (\frac{\sqrt{3}}{2}+1)b^2 = 8$$

$$\Rightarrow \quad b^2 = \frac{8}{\frac{\sqrt{3}}{2}+1}$$

$$\Rightarrow \quad b = 2.07$$

4. **Solution:** $1\frac{7}{8}$.

Let t be the minutes it takes Susan to climb up the moving escalator.
We have:

$$45t + 75t = 225 \qquad \Rightarrow \qquad t = \frac{225}{120} = \frac{15}{8} = 1\frac{7}{8}.$$

5. **Solution:** 6666.

There are $\binom{9}{4} \times 4! = 3024$ ways to select 4 different digits from the given 9 digits

to form a 4-digit number.

Assuming that we selected 1, 2, 3, and 4, the total number of 4-digit numbers will
be $4 \times 3 \times 2 \times 1 = 24$.

The sum of all 24 numbers is

$$S_1 = \frac{4 \times 3 \times 2 \times 1}{4} \times (1+2+3+4)(1000+100+10+1) = 6666 \times (1+2+3+4).$$

If we selected the digits 2, 3, 4, and 5, the sum would be

$$S_2 = \frac{4 \times 3 \times 2 \times 1}{4} \times (2+3+4+5)(1000+100+10+1) = 6666 \times (2+3+4+5)$$

Similarly, we have,

$$S_3 = \frac{4 \times 3 \times 2 \times 1}{4} \times (3+4+5+6)(1000+100+10+1) = 6666 \times (3+4+5+6)$$

……………..

If we selected the digits a_1, a_2, a_3, a_4, the sum would be

$$S_n = \frac{4 \times 3 \times 2 \times 1}{4} \times (a_1 + a_2 + a_3 + a_4)(1000 + 100 + 10 + 1) = 6666 \times (a_1 + a_2 + a_3 + a_4)$$

The greatest common factor of all such sums is 6666.

6. Solution: $\dfrac{\sqrt{13} + 2}{2}$.

Let A be the surface area of the cone and V be the volume of the cone.

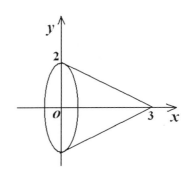

A equals Area of cone + Area of base, or $\pi r s + \pi r^2$.

$$V = \frac{1}{3} \pi r^2 h.$$

Dividing A by V, we get

$$\frac{A}{V} = \frac{\pi r s + \pi r^2}{\frac{1}{3}\pi r^2 h} = \frac{3(s+r)}{rh}$$

$$= \frac{3 \times (\sqrt{3^2 + 2^2}) + 2)}{2 \times 3} = \frac{\sqrt{13} + 2}{2}$$

7. Solution: 35.

If the product is fixed, the greatest sum is obtained by having the numbers be far apart as possible. The following arrangement gives the maximum sum:

$$2^5 \times 3^5 = 6 \times 6 \times 6 \times 6 \times 6 \times 1 \times 1 \times 1 \times 1 \times 1$$

The largest possible sum is:
$$6 + 6 + 6 + 6 + 6 + 1 + 1 + 1 + 1 + 1 = 5 \times 6 + 5 \times 1 = 35.$$

8. Solution: 1/6

Since $AB = 2AC = 3AE = 4DB$, we can let $AB = $ LCM $(2, 3, 4) = 12$. It follows that $AC = 6$, $AE = 4$, $DB = 3$, and $EC = 2$.
The probability that x between E and C is $EC/AB = 2/12 = 1/6$.

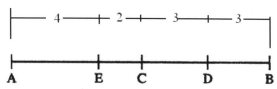

9. **Solution:** 23.
The problem is the same as finding the remainder when 3^{1993} is divided by 100, or in other words, finding the last two digits of 3^{1993}.

We know that $\phi(100) = 40$ and $3^{\phi(100)} \equiv 1 \pmod{100}$.

So $3^{1993} = 3^{49 \times 40 + 33} \equiv 3^{33} \pmod{100}$
$3^{33} \equiv R \pmod{100}$ can be written as:
$3^{33} \equiv R_1 \pmod{25}$ (1)   and
$3^{33} \equiv R_2 \pmod 4$ (2)

Note that 25 and 4 are relatively prime.

From (2), we have
$(-1)^{33} \equiv -1 \equiv 3 \pmod 4$, so $R_1 = 3$.
$3^{33} \equiv R_2 \pmod{25}$
$\Rightarrow \quad (3^3)^{11} \equiv R_2 \pmod{25}$
$\Rightarrow \quad (2)^{11} \equiv R_2 \pmod{25}$
$\Rightarrow \quad 2^{11} = 1024 \times 2 \equiv -2 \equiv 23 \pmod{25}$

So $R_2 = 23$.

The first common term for R_1 and R_2 is 23 (note $3+4+4+4+4+4=23$).
So $n = 23$ is the answer.

10. **Solution:** $6 - 3\sqrt[3]{4}$.

As shown in the figure, the two pyramids are similar. Let the volume of the large pyramid be V_L and the smaller be V_S and let x be the distance from the plane to the base of the pyramid.

We have:

$$\frac{V_L}{V_S} = (\frac{6}{6-x})^3$$

$$\Rightarrow \quad \frac{2}{1} = (\frac{6}{6-x})^3$$

$$\Rightarrow \quad 2 = (\frac{6}{6-x})^3$$

$$\Rightarrow \quad \sqrt[3]{2} = \frac{6}{6-x}$$

$$\Rightarrow \quad 6-x = \frac{6}{\sqrt[3]{2}}$$

$$\Rightarrow \quad x = 6 - \frac{6}{\sqrt[3]{2}} = 6 - \frac{6\sqrt[3]{2^2}}{\sqrt[3]{2} \times \sqrt[3]{2^2}} = 6 - 3\sqrt[3]{4}.$$

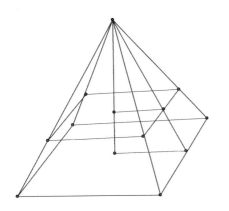
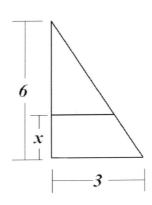

1995 National Team Round Solutions

1. **Solution:** 14%.

To probability that the will land inside the square but not inside the inner circle, we need to find the area within the square that is not part of the inner circle.

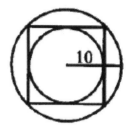

The diameter of the outer circle, or 20, is also the hypotenuse of an isosceles right triangle whose leg is equal to the side of the square. It follows that the length of a side of the square is $10\sqrt{2}$.

The radius of the smaller circle is half of the length of the square, or $5\sqrt{2}$.

The probability is:

$$P = \frac{(2\sqrt{10})^2 - \pi(5\sqrt{2})^2}{\pi(10)} = 14\%.$$

2. **Solution:** 6.

There are 5 possible configurations as shown below. We have 1, 5, 6, 8, and 10 distinct lines for the following cases, respectively. The median is 6.

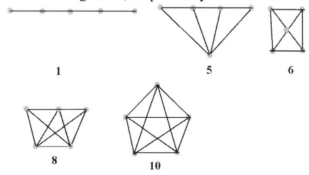

3. **Solution:** 12 sets.

Let three binomials be $m_1a + n_1b$, $m_2a + n_2b$, and $m_2a + n_2b$.

The sum will be $m_1a + n_1b + m_2a + n_2b + m_2a + n_2b = (m_1 + m_2 + m_3)a + (n_1 + n_2 + n_3)b$.

We know that

$m_1 + m_2 + m_3 = 4$ $\Rightarrow$ $(2, 1, 1)$

$n_1 + n_2 + n_3 = 8$ $\Rightarrow$ $(6, 1, 1), (5, 2, 1), (4, 3, 1), (4, 2, 2), (3, 3, 2)$

Case 1. $\begin{pmatrix} 2a+6b \\ a+b \\ a+b \end{pmatrix}, \begin{pmatrix} 2a+b \\ a+6b \\ a+b \end{pmatrix} = \begin{pmatrix} 2a+b \\ a+b \\ a+6b \end{pmatrix}$ $\Rightarrow$ 2 distinct sets.

Case 2. $\begin{pmatrix} 2a+5b \\ a+2b \\ a+b \end{pmatrix}, \begin{pmatrix} 2a+2b \\ a+5b \\ a+b \end{pmatrix}, \begin{pmatrix} 2a+b \\ a+2b \\ a+5b \end{pmatrix}$ $\Rightarrow$ 3 distinct sets.

Case 3. $\begin{pmatrix} 2a+4b \\ a+3b \\ a+b \end{pmatrix}, \begin{pmatrix} 2a+3b \\ a+4b \\ a+b \end{pmatrix}, \begin{pmatrix} 2a+b \\ a+3b \\ a+4b \end{pmatrix}$ $\Rightarrow$ 3 distinct sets.

Case 4. $\begin{pmatrix} 2a+4b \\ a+2b \\ a+2b \end{pmatrix}, \begin{pmatrix} 2a+2b \\ a+4b \\ a+2b \end{pmatrix} = \begin{pmatrix} 2a+2b \\ a+2b \\ a+4b \end{pmatrix}$ $\Rightarrow$ 2 distinct sets.

Case 5. $\begin{pmatrix} 2a+3b \\ a+3b \\ a+2b \end{pmatrix}, \begin{pmatrix} 2a+2b \\ a+3b \\ a+3b \end{pmatrix} = \begin{pmatrix} 2a+3b \\ a+2b \\ a+3b \end{pmatrix}$ $\Rightarrow$ 2 distinct sets.

In total there are $2 + 3 + 3 + 2 + 2 = 12$ sets.

4. **Solution:** 43 miles per hour.
We are given that the wheels turn 400 times in 1 minute and have diameters of three feet. In one turn, the wheels travel 3π.

$$\frac{400 \times 3\pi \text{ feet}}{1 \text{ minute}} = \frac{400 \times 3\pi \text{ feet}}{\dfrac{1}{60} \text{ hour}} = \frac{400 \times 3\pi \times 60 \text{ feet}}{1 \text{ hour}}$$

$$= \frac{\dfrac{400 \times 3\pi \times 60 \text{ miles}}{5280}}{1 \text{ hour}} = 43 \text{ miles per hour}$$

5. **Solution:** 42.75

The length of the rungs on the ladder, a_1 to a_n, consist of an arithmetic sequence with the first term $a_1 = 24$, the last term $a_9 = 18$, and $n = 9$.

a_5 can be calculated by taking the average of the first and last term:

$$a_5 = \frac{a_1 + a_9}{2} = \frac{24 + 18}{2} = 21.$$

Next, we calculate the common difference d in the arithmetic sequence:

$$a_9 = a_1 + (9 - 1)d \qquad \Rightarrow \qquad d = -3/4.$$

$$a_5 = a_4 + d \qquad \Rightarrow \qquad a_4 = a_5 - d = 21 - (-\frac{3}{4}) = 21.75$$

The sum is equal to $a_4 + a_5 = 21 + 21.75 = 42.75$.

6. **Solution:** 504.

Case I: The thousand digit is 8:

$\underline{1} \times \underline{8} \times \underline{7} \times \underline{4} = 224$ (The unit digit has 4 choices since it must be even and not 8 and can only be 0, 2, 4, or 6)

Case II: The thousand digit is 9:

$\underline{1} \times \underline{8} \times \underline{7} \times \underline{5} = 280$ (The unit digit has 5 choices since it must be even and can be 0, 2, 4, 6 or 8).

The answer is 504.

7. **Solution:** 6.

The number of distinct star polygons for $n = 36$ equals:

$$S(n) = \frac{\phi(n)}{2} = \frac{\phi(36)}{2} = 6.$$

Note: $S(n)$ denotes the number of different star polygons with n points that can be constructed with one continuous path and $S(n) = \phi(n)/2$, where $\phi(n)$ is called the Euler's totient function.

8. Solution: 7.
Ankur can cut out $4 \times 7 = 28$ whole cookies from the rectangular dough. The area remaining is:

$$10 \times 18.5 - 28 \times \pi(\frac{2.5}{2})^2 \approx 47.555.$$

Since one cookie requires the space of 2.5×2.5, Ankur can cut out

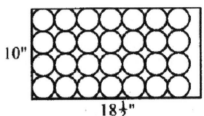

$$\frac{47.55}{2.5 \times 2.5} \approx 7.61 \text{ cookies from the next rolling.}$$

The greatest number of whole cookies is $\lfloor 7.71 \rfloor = 7$.

9. Solution: 18.

	x years ago	Now
Sally's age	$24 - x$	24
Allie's age	$A - x$	A

$$\begin{cases} 24 - x = A \\ 2(A - x) = 24 \end{cases} \Rightarrow A = 18$$

10. Solution: 761.

Letting $\dfrac{n(n+1)}{2} = 723$, we get $n = \left\lfloor \dfrac{-1 + \sqrt{1 + 4 \times 2 \times 723}}{2} \right\rfloor = 37$.

When $n = 37$, the first number in 37th row is $\dfrac{n(n+1)}{2} = \dfrac{37 \times 38}{2} = 703$.

When $n = 38$, the first number in 38th row is $\dfrac{38 \times 39}{2} = 741$.

Since $723 = 703 + 20$, 723 is 20 away from the beginning of the row. The number directly above the number 723 is 20 away from the beginning of the next row, or $41 + 20 = 761$.

1996 National Team Round Solutions:

1. Solution: $0.71.
Let x be the fixed price of an empty box, y be the price per ounce of cereal.

We are given that
$$x + 12y = 3.35 \qquad (1)$$
$$x + 18y = 4.67 \qquad (2)$$

$(1) \times 3 - (2) \times 2$: $x = \$0.71$.

2. Solution: $10\dfrac{1}{12}$.

$$x - [x] = \frac{1}{[x]} \qquad (1)$$
$$x = [x] + \{x\} \qquad (2)$$

where $\{x\}$ is the decimal part of x.

Substituting (2) into (1), we get
$$[x] + \{x\} - [x] = \frac{1}{[x]}$$
$$\Rightarrow \{x\} = \frac{1}{[x]}$$
$$\Rightarrow [x]\{x\} = 1 \qquad (3)$$

(3) indicates that for any number, its integer part is the same as the denominator of the decimal part, and when its integer part is multiplied by its decimal part, the result is 1.

Since we want to find the three smallest positive solutions, we first test out some numbers.
(1) tells us that $[x] \neq 1$ because if $[x] = 1$, then from (1), we get $x = 2$, which is a contradiction.

So we start with $[x] = 2$.

31

$x_1 = 2\dfrac{1}{2}:$ $2 \times \dfrac{1}{2}$ (works)

Next we have $[x] = 3$.

$x_2 = 3\dfrac{1}{3}:$ $3 \times \dfrac{1}{3}$ (works)

Next we have $[x] = 4$.

$x_2 = 4\dfrac{1}{4}:$ $4 \times \dfrac{1}{4}$ (works)

The sum of the three smallest positive solutions is

$$2\dfrac{1}{2} + 3\dfrac{1}{3} + 4\dfrac{1}{4} = 10\dfrac{1}{12}.$$

3. **Solution:** 6/25.

m and n have 5 possible values, and so there are a total of 25 points in S.

For a line with the slope 1, we have $(1 + 2 + 4 + 2 + 1) = 10$ such pairs of points.
For a line with the slope -1, we also have 10 such pairs of points.
For example, B is the midpoint of AC, C is the midpoint of BD, D is the midpoint of CE, and C is the midpoint of AE (ie. 4 pairs).

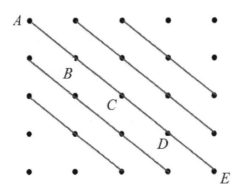

For a line with the slope 2, we have $(1 + 1 + 1) = 3$ such pairs of points.

For a line with the slope −2, we also have 3 such pairs of points.

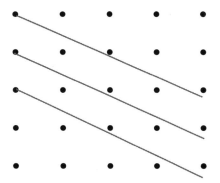

For a line with the slope 1/2, we have $(1 + 1 + 1) = 3$ such pairs of points.
For a line with the slope −1/2, we also have 3 such pairs of points.

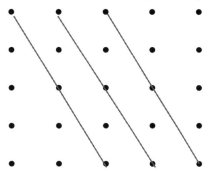

For a line with the slope 0, we have $4 \times 5 = 20$ such pairs of points
For a line with the slope infinitely large, we also have 20 such pairs of points.

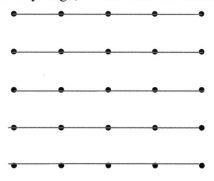

In total, there are $20 + 6 + 6 + 20 + 20 = 72$ pairs of points.

There are $\binom{25}{2} = 300$ total ways to choose two points from the set of 25.

Thus, the probability is $72/300 = 72/300 = 6/25$.

4. **Solution:** 6 ways.

12	20	21	21	22	22	22
13	19	20	21	22	22	23
14	17	20	21	22	22	24
14	18	19	21	22	22	24
15	16	19	21	22	22	25
15	17	18	21	22	22	25

Note The correct answer is 6 (not 7 as published in some places).

5. **Solution:** 0.58.
Let the outer circle's radius be x, and the radius of the inner circle be y.

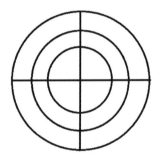

Since each region is $1/12^{\text{th}}$ of the total region, looking at a quarter of the smallest circle, we have

$$\frac{\pi x^2}{12} = \frac{\pi y^2}{4} \qquad \Rightarrow \qquad y = \frac{\sqrt{3}}{3}x$$

The ratio of the radius of the innermost of the three concentric circles to the radius

of the outer circle is $\dfrac{\dfrac{\sqrt{3}}{3}x}{x} = \dfrac{\sqrt{3}}{3} \approx 0.58$.

6. **Solution:** 813.
We see that the digits 3 and 8 are both in the number 836 and 983, so n must contain the digits 3 and 8.

8	3	6
3	1	5
9	8	3

Only 813 follows the given conditions.

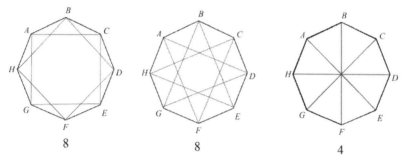

7. Solution: $\dfrac{31}{95}$

Label the octagon $ABCDEFG$. There are 20 diagonals in all, 5 diagonals coming out from each vertex. The diagonals are of three types:

Case 1:
Diagonals that skip over only one vertex, such as AC or AG. There are 8 such diagonals.

The probability that Emily and Tim have both selected one of these diagonals is:

$$P_1 = \frac{8}{20} \times \frac{7}{19}.$$

Case 2:
Diagonals that skip two vertices, such as AD or AF. There are 8 such diagonals.
The probability that Emily and Tim have both selected one of these diagonals is:

$$P_2 = \frac{8}{20} \times \frac{7}{19}.$$

Case 3:
Diagonals that cross to the opposite vertex, such as AE. There are 8 such diagonals.

The probability that Emily and Tim have both selected one of these diagonals is:

$$P_3 = \frac{4}{20} \times \frac{3}{19}.$$

The total probability is $P = P_1 + P_3 + P_3 = \dfrac{8}{20} \times \dfrac{7}{19} + \dfrac{8}{20} \times \dfrac{7}{19} + \dfrac{4}{20} \times \dfrac{3}{19} = \dfrac{31}{95}.$

8. Solution: 6570.

The first ten rows each contain 20 seats, so the first ten rows contain a total of 10 × 20 = 200 seats.

The number of seats from 11th row to 80th row in each row form an arithmetic sequence, where the first term is 22, the common difference is 2, and the number of rows is 70.

The sum of the arithmetic sequence is
$$S = na_1 + \frac{n(n-1)d}{2} = 70 \times 22 + \frac{70(70-1)2}{2} = 6370.$$
The total number of seats in the auditorium is is 200 + 6370 = 6570.

9. Solution: 180.

The four smallest positive integers with an even number of distinct factors are 2, 3, 5, and 6. Their product is 2 × 3 × 5 × 6 = 180.

10. Solution: $\dfrac{13}{6}$.

Since we know that $x + 9$ is the longest side of triangle ABC, we have both $x + 4 < x + 9$, which does not give us any useful information and
$3x < x + 9$
$\Rightarrow \qquad 2x < 9$

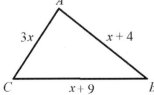

36

$$\Rightarrow \quad x < \frac{9}{2}.$$

By the Triangle Inequality, which says that the sum of two sides of a triangle must be greater than the third side, we have:

$$x + 9 < x + 4 + 3x$$
$$\Rightarrow \quad 3x > 5$$
$$\Rightarrow \quad x > \frac{5}{3}.$$

The answer is $\dfrac{9}{2} - \dfrac{5}{3} = \dfrac{17}{6}$.

1997 National Team Round Solutions:

1. Solution: 8.

$144 = 12^2 = (2^4 \times 3^2) = (3 \times 6 \times 8)$.

The three integers are 3, 6, and 8 with the greatest integer being 8.

2. Solution: $\dfrac{175}{256}$.

Step	Fractional part
1 (Change 1)	1/4
2	$1/4 + 3 \times (1/4)^2$.
3	$1/4 + 3 \times (1/4)^2 + 3^2 \times (1/4)^3$
4	$1/4 + 3 \times (1/4)^2 + 3^2 \times (1/4)^3 + 3^3 \times (1/4)^4$

After four changes, the fractional part that is shaded is $\dfrac{175}{256}$.

3. Solution: 2519

Let the integer be x. We are given that

$$x \equiv 4 \quad \mod 5 \tag{1}$$
$$x \equiv 5 \quad \mod 6 \tag{2}$$
$$x \equiv 6 \quad \mod 7 \tag{3}$$
$$x \equiv 7 \quad \mod 8 \tag{4}$$
$$x \equiv 8 \quad \mod 9 \tag{5}$$

(1) to (5) can be written as:

$$x + 1 \equiv 0 \quad \mod 5 \tag{6}$$
$$x + 1 \equiv 0 \quad \mod 6 \tag{7}$$
$$x + 1 \equiv 0 \quad \mod 7 \tag{8}$$
$$x + 1 \equiv 0 \quad \mod 8 \tag{9}$$
$$x + 1 \equiv 0 \quad \mod 9 \tag{10}$$

(6) to (10) can be written as:

$$x + 1 \equiv 0 \quad \mod \text{LCM } (5, 6, 7, 8, 9) \text{ or}$$

$x + 1 \equiv 0 \qquad \text{mod } 2520$

The smallest value for x is $2520 - 1 = 2519$.

4. Solution: 11.2 (units)

Draw the circumcircle of triangle XYZ and the two diameters of the circle. Label all the line segments as shown in the figure to the right.

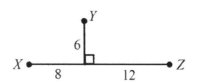

We see that $TM = NO = 2$.

$XT \times TZ = YT \times TP$

$\Rightarrow 8 \times 12 = 6 \times TP$

$\Rightarrow TP = 16$.

It follows that $YP = 22$ and $NP = 11$.

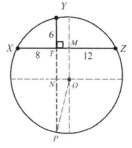

Applying Pythagorean Theorem to triangle NPO, we get

$OP^2 = NO^2 + NP^2 = 2^2 + 11^1 = 125$.

$OP = \sqrt{125} = 5\sqrt{5} \approx 11.2$.

5. Solution: 120.

Case 1: Tens digit is 9.

If the sum of the first and last digits is 8, we have 8 choices for the first digit (8, 7, 6, 5, 4, 3, 2, or 1) and one choice for the last digit.

If the sum of the first and last digits is 7, we have 7 choices for the first digit (7, 6, 5, 4, 3, 2, or 1) and one choice for the last digit.

If the sum of the first and last digits is 6, we have 6 choices for the first digit (6, 5, 4, 3, 2, or 1) and one choice for the last digit.

If the sum of the first and last digits is 5, we have 5 choices for the first digit (5, 4, 3, 2, or 1) and one choice for the last digit.

If the sum of the first and last digits is 4, we have 4 choices for the first digit (4, 3, 2, or 1) and one choice for the last digit.

If the sum of the first and last digits is 3, we have 3 choices for the first digit (3, 2, or 1) and one choice for the last digit.

If the sum of the first and last digits is 2, we have 2 choices for the first digit (2, or 1) and one choice for the last digit.

If the sum of the first and last is 1, we have 1 choice for the first digit (1) and one choice for the last digit.

In total, there are $8 + 7 + 6 + 6 + 4 + 3 + 2 + 1 = 36$ such numbers for this case.

Case 2: Tens digit is 8.
We have $36 - 8 = 28$ such numbers.

Similarly, when the tens digit is 7, 6, 5, 4, 3, 2, we have 21, 15, 10, 6, 3, and 1 such numbers, respectively.

The answer is $36 + 28 + 21 + 15 + 10 + 6 + 3 + 1 = 120$.

6. Solution: 30π.
The volumes of two cylinders are
$V_1 = \pi \times w^2 l = \pi \times 5^2 \times 3 = 75\pi$.
$V_2 = \pi \times l^2 w = \pi \times 3^2 \times 5 = 45\pi$

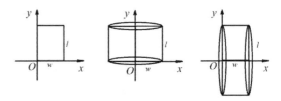

The positive difference is
$75\pi - 45\pi = 30\pi$.

7. Solution: 5.
Since the numbers must be less than 400, the first digit can only be 2 or 3.

Since each of the three digits is prime, the middle digit can be 2, 3, 5, 7.

Since the number is prime, the last digit can be 3 or 7.
In total, there can be $2 \times 4 \times 2 = 16$ possible numbers, listed as follows:

223	227	323	327
233	237	333	337
252	257	353	357
273	277	373	377

Removing each number such that the sum of its digits is not prime, we are left with 223, 227, 353, 373, 337, and 377.

Since $377 = 13 \times 29$ is not a prime, we remove it from the set, giving us 5 numbers that satisfy each of the conditions.

8. **Solution:** 139 (square centimeters).
Given the description in the problem, we can draw the square pyramid as shown.

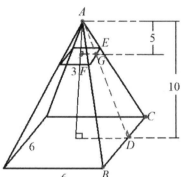

$AD = \sqrt{10^2 + 3^2} = \sqrt{109}$.

Right triangles AEF and ACB are similar.

Since $BC/EF = 6/3 = 2/1$, $AG = DG = \dfrac{\sqrt{109}}{2}$.

$$S_{BCEF} = \frac{(EF + BC) \times DG}{2} = \frac{(3+6) \times \dfrac{\sqrt{109}}{2}}{2} = \frac{9\sqrt{109}}{4}$$

The surface area of the frustum is

$$3 \times 3 + 6 \times 6 + 4 S_{BCEF} = 45 + 4 \times \frac{9\sqrt{109}}{4} \approx 139.$$

9. **Solution:** 0.61.
Since we want to find a ratio, we can let the radius of the circle be 6. We label the figure as shown and connect BD, DC, and CB.

Note that $AB = BD = DC = CB = 6$ since they are all radii of the circle, and triangle BCD is an equilateral triangle. Thus $\angle DBC = 60°$, and the area of the

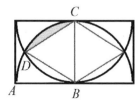

triangle DCB is $\dfrac{1}{4} \times \sqrt{3} \times (DC)^2 = 9\sqrt{3}$.

The area of the sector DCB is $\dfrac{\pi \times 6^2}{6} = 6\pi$.

It follows that the shaded area is $6\pi - 9\sqrt{3}$.

The area that is inside the rectangle and also inside both semicircles is $4 \times (6\pi - 9\sqrt{3}) + 2 \times 9\sqrt{3} = 24\pi - 18\sqrt{3}$.

The probability that a point randomly selected inside the rectangle will also be inside both semicircles is $\dfrac{24\pi - 18\sqrt{3}}{12 \times 6} = 0.61$.

10. **Solution:** 1200 triangles.

At most, there can be $\dbinom{21}{3} = 1330$ possible triangles.

At 3 points selected from 5 points on a line will not form a triangle. There are $3\dbinom{7}{3} = 105$ ways to do so.

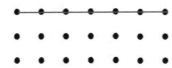

Any 3 points selected from 3 points on a line will not form a triangle. There are $7\dbinom{3}{3} = 7$ ways to do so.

Any 3 points selected from 3 points on a line will not form a triangle. There are $10\dbinom{3}{3} = 10$ ways to do so.

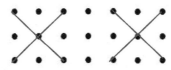

Any 3 points selected from 3 points on a line will not form a triangle. There are $6\binom{3}{3} = 6$ ways to do so.

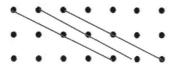

Any 3 points selected from 3 points on a line will not form a triangle. There are $2\binom{3}{3} = 2$ ways to do so.

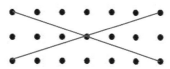

The total number of triangles that can be formed is $1330 - 105 - 7 - 10 - 6 - 2 = 1200$.

1998 National Team Round Solutions

1. **Solution:** 29.

Let g be the number of girls and b be the number of boys in the class. Note that

$66\dfrac{2}{3}\% = \dfrac{200}{300}$ and $71\dfrac{3}{7}\% = \dfrac{50}{700}$. Since five girls do not wear watches, we have

$\dfrac{200}{300}g = g - 5 \Rightarrow \quad g = 15.$

Since the same number of boys and girls wear watches,

$\dfrac{2}{3} \times 15 = \dfrac{50}{700}b \qquad \Rightarrow \qquad b = 14.$

The total number of boys and girls in the class is $15 + 14 = 29$.

2. **Solution:** 5.77.

Method 1:

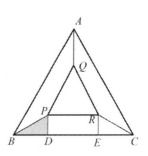

Since AB = 20 cm, then $S_{\Delta ABC} = \dfrac{\sqrt{3}}{4} \times 20^2 = 100\sqrt{3}$.

Given that the four interior regions $AQPB$, $AQRC$, $BPRC$ and

QPR all have the same area, $S_{\Delta PQR} = \dfrac{1}{4} \times S_{\Delta ABC} = 25\sqrt{3}$.

It follows that

$\dfrac{PR^2}{4} \times \sqrt{3} = 25\sqrt{3} \qquad \Rightarrow \qquad PR = 10.$

The area of trapezoid $PRCB$ can be written as

$S_{PRCD} = \dfrac{(PR + BC)}{2} \times PD = 25\sqrt{3}$

$\Rightarrow \qquad \dfrac{(10 + 20)}{2} \times PD = 25\sqrt{3}$

$\Rightarrow \qquad PD = \dfrac{25\sqrt{3}}{15} = \dfrac{5\sqrt{3}}{3}.$

Looking at the $30 - 60 - 90°$ right triangle PDB, we get

$$PB = 2PD = \frac{2 \times 5\sqrt{3}}{3} \approx 5.77 .$$

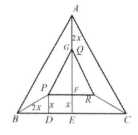

Method 2:

In equilateral triangle $\triangle ABC$, $AE = \frac{\sqrt{3}}{2} \times AB = 10\sqrt{3}$.

In equilateral triangle $\triangle PQR$, $QF = \frac{\sqrt{3}}{2} \times PR = 5\sqrt{3}$.

$AE = AG + GF + EF$

$\Rightarrow \quad 2x + 5\sqrt{3} + x = 10\sqrt{3}$

$\Rightarrow \quad 3x = 5\sqrt{3}$

$\Rightarrow \quad x = \frac{5\sqrt{3}}{3}$

$\Rightarrow \quad PB = 2x = 2 \times \frac{5\sqrt{3}}{3} \approx 5.77 .$

3. **Solution:** 36.

Since x and y are positive integers and $37x + 73y = 2016$,

$2016 - 73y \equiv 0$	mod 37
$\Rightarrow 18 - 36y \equiv 0$	mod 37
$\Rightarrow 36y \equiv 18$	mod 37
$\Rightarrow 2y \equiv 1$	mod 37
$\Rightarrow 2y \equiv 1 + 37 = 38$	mod 37
$\Rightarrow y \equiv 19$	mod 37

When $y = 19$, we have

$37x = 2016 - 73y = 2016 - 73 \times 19 = 629$

$\Rightarrow \quad x = 17.$

The answer is $17 + 19 = 36$.

4. **Solution:** 25.

Let x be the distance from point A to the other wall.

Applying Pythagorean Theorem to triangle ABC, we have
$$(37-x)^2 + 35^2 = 37^2$$
$$\Rightarrow \quad (37-x)^2 = 37^2 - 35^2 = 144 = 12^2$$
$$\Rightarrow \quad 37 - x = 12$$
$$\Rightarrow \quad x = 37 - 12 = 25 .$$
A is 25 inches away from the other wall.

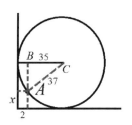

5. **Solution:** 6 minutes.

The total time it took for Bob to complete the race was $\dfrac{12}{12} + \dfrac{12}{8} = \dfrac{5}{2} = 2.5$ hours.

Let the total time it took for Bill be t.

$$\frac{t}{2} \times 12 + \frac{t}{2} \times 8 = 24 \quad \Rightarrow \quad t = 2.4 \text{ hours.}$$

Bill won the race by $2.5 - 2.4 = 0.1$ hours $= 6$ minutes.

6. **Solution:** $\dfrac{13}{40}$.

Case 1: The marble selected from the mayonnaise jar is red and the marble selected from the jelly jar is also red:
$$P_1 = \frac{6}{10} \times \frac{2+1}{7+1} = \frac{9}{40} .$$

Case 2: The marble selected from the mayonnaise jar is blue and the marble selected from the jelly jar is red:
$$P_2 = \frac{4}{10} \times \frac{2}{7+1} = \frac{1}{10} .$$

The total probability is $P = P_1 + P_2 = \dfrac{9}{40} + \dfrac{1}{10} = \dfrac{13}{40}$.

7. **Solution:** 12.81 (inches).
We unfold the box as shown.
The least distance from A to B is
$$AB = \sqrt{8^2 + 10^2} = \sqrt{164} \approx 12.81 .$$

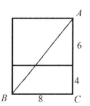

8. Solution: -99.

In order for the cube of an integer to have the same units digit as the integer, the units digit must be 1, 4, 5, 6, or 9.

The least two–digit integer is -99. We see that $(-99)^3 = -970299$, which indeed has the same tens and units digits as -99.

9. Solution: 23.

The smallest positive integer that can be expressed as the sum of eight cubes of positive integers is $15 = 2^3 + 1^3 + 1^3 + 1^3 + 1^3 + 1^3 + 1^3 + 1^3$.

The smallest positive integer that cannot be expressed as the sum of eight or fewer cubes of positive integers is
$23 = 2^3 + 2^3 + 1^3 + 1^3 + 1^3 + 1^3 + 1^3 + 1^3 + 1^3$, which needs nine cubes of positive integers.

Note that 24 can be expressed as the sum of eight or fewer cubes of positive integers:
$24 = 2^3 + 2^3 + 1^3 + 1^3 + 1^3 + 1^3 + 1^3 + 1^3 + 1^3 + 1^3 = 2^3 + 2^3 + 2^3$.

23 is the answer.

Note that every positive integer is a sum of no more than 9 positive cubes and the only integers requiring nine positive cubes are 23 and 239. This topic is called "Waring's problem".

10. Solution: 135.

The diagonal passes through $N = m + n - \text{GCF}(m, n) = 81 + 63 - 9 = 135$ tiles.

1999 National Team Round Solutions

1. **Solution:** 60 paths.
We can solve this problem using the method of water pipes, where the number of paths to a vertex is equal to the sum of the number of paths to the left adjacent vertex and the number of paths to the right adjacent vertex.

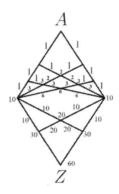

2. **Solution:** 9.6 (inches).
Let the center of the circle be O. Connect BO and AO and draw $BC \perp CO$.
The area of the inner circular pane is $\pi \times r^2 = 16\pi$.

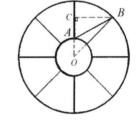

Since all nine regions have the same area, the area of the large circle is $16\pi \times 9 = 144\pi$, resulting in the radius OB to be 12.

Angle COB is $360°/8 = 45°$.

Therefore triangle OCB is an isosceles right triangle and $\sqrt{2}\,OC = OB$

$$\Rightarrow \quad OC = \frac{12}{\sqrt{2}} = 6\sqrt{2}.$$

It follows that $CA = OC - AO = 6\sqrt{2} - 4$.

Applying Pythagorean Theorem to triangle ABC, we get
$$AB^2 = AC^2 + BC^2 = (6\sqrt{2} - 4)^2 + (6\sqrt{2})^2 \approx 9.6.$$

3. **Solution:** $\dfrac{7}{20}$.

$$\frac{1}{x^2}+\frac{1}{y^2}=\frac{x^2+y^2}{(xy)^2}=\frac{x^2+y^2-2xy+2xy}{(xy)^2}=\frac{(x-y)^2+2xy}{(xy)^2}=\frac{100+40}{400}=\frac{140}{400}$$

$$=\frac{7}{20}.$$

4. **Solution:** 48.

$$s=\frac{6+50+52}{2}=54.$$

From Heron's Formula,

$$S_{\Delta}=\sqrt{54(54-6)(54-50)(54-52)}=\sqrt{54(48)(4)(2)}=144.$$

Let x be the length of the altitude to the shortest side of the triangle.

The area of the triangle is

$$\frac{6x}{2}=144$$

$$\Rightarrow \qquad x=48.$$

5. **Solution:** 9.78.

We label ABC and connect AC, BC, and AB as shown.
ABC is an equilateral triangle.

$$S_{\Delta ABC}=\frac{\sqrt{3}}{4}AB^2=\frac{9\sqrt{3}}{4}.$$

The area of the sector of CAB is $S_{CAB}=\frac{1}{6}\pi\times AC^2=\frac{3\pi}{2}.$

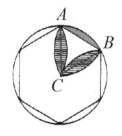

It follows that the area of the green shaded region is

$$S_{CAB}-S_{\Delta ABC}=\frac{3\pi}{2}-\frac{9\sqrt{3}}{4}.$$

The green shaded region is equivalent to $1/12^{\text{th}}$ of the total shaded region shown in the problem's figure.

Therefore, the total shaded region is equal to

$$12 \times (S_{CAB} - S_{\triangle ABC}) = 12 \times (\frac{3\pi}{2} - \frac{9\sqrt{3}}{4}) \approx 9.78.$$

6. **Solution:** 49.
Method 1:

Solving for x, we get: $x = \dfrac{12y}{y-12} = 12 + \dfrac{12^2}{y-12}$

Since x is a positive integer, $y - 12$ must be a factor of $12^2 = 2^4 \times 3^2$ which has the following 15 factors:

         1, 2, 3, 4, 6, 8, 9, **12,** 16, 18, 24, 36, 48, 72, 144.

The smallest value for $x + y$ is obtained when x and y are as close to each other as possible. For example, when $x = 24$ and $y = 24$, $x + y = 48$ will be the smallest value possible. Because x and y must be different, we can't have them as the same, but the next pair in line will suffice.

Letting $y - 12 = 9$ (or 16), we get $y = 21$ and $x = 28$ (or $y = 28$ and $x = 21$). Therefore $28 + 21 = 49$ is the answer.

We can easily verify this answer by looking at the complete list (156, 13), (84, 14), (60, 15), (48, 16), (36,18), (30, 20), (28, 21), (24, 24), and confirming that 49 is the smallest sum.

Method 2:
The given equation can be written as:
$12y + 12x = xy$

$\Rightarrow \quad xy - 12x - 12x = 0$

$\Rightarrow \quad (x - 12)(y - 12) = 144$

The smallest value for $x + y$ is obtained when x and y are as close as possible.

Since $x \neq y$, we are not able to write $(x - 12)(y - 12) = 12 \times 12$ but we can say that $(x - 12)(y - 12) = 9 \times 16$.

Letting $y - 12 = 9$ (or 16), we get $y = 21$ and $x = 28$ (or $y = 28$ and $x = 21$).

Therefore $28 + 21 = 49$ is the answer.

7. Solution: $\dfrac{2}{3}$.

Folding the paper in such a way divides the paper into two pieces with equal area.

$S_{BAEF} = S_{FCDB} \Rightarrow \qquad S_{BAEF} = \dfrac{2 \times 1}{2} = 1$.

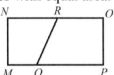

$S_{NMQR} = S_{RQPO} \Rightarrow \qquad S_{NMQR} = \dfrac{1 \times 3}{2} = \dfrac{3}{2}$.

The answer is $\dfrac{S_{BAEF}}{S_{NMQR}} = \dfrac{1}{\dfrac{3}{2}} = \dfrac{2}{3}$.

8. Solution: $4\sqrt{13}$.

We unfold the cylindrical pole as shown in the figure.

Applying Pythagorean Theorem to right triangle ABC:
$AC = \sqrt{2^2 + 3^2} = \sqrt{13}$.

The minimum number of feet in the length of the rope is
$4AC = 4 \times \sqrt{13} = 4\sqrt{13}$

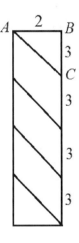

9. Solution: 5.

We can get $n = 4, 7, 10, \ldots$ by partitioning in the following way:

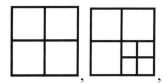

We can get $n = 6, 9, 12, 15, \ldots$ by partitioning in the following way:

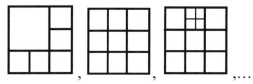

We can get $n = 8, 11, 14, \ldots$ by partitioning in the following way:

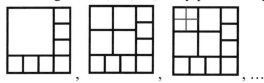

We can get $n = 11, 14, 17$ by partitioning in the following way:

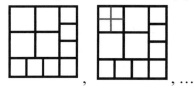

We are able to partition the square into n pieces where

$$n \equiv 0 \bmod 3 \quad (n = 3, 6, 9, 12, \ldots) \tag{1}$$
$$n \equiv 1 \bmod 3 \quad (n = 4, 7, 10, 13, \ldots) \tag{2}$$
$$n \equiv 2 \bmod 3 \quad (n = 8, 11, 14, \ldots) \tag{3}$$

From (3), we see that we are not able to $n = 2$ or $n = 2 + 3 = 5$. The greatest integer n such that a square cannot be partitioned into n smaller squares is 5.

10. Solution: 2519
Let the integer be x.

$$x \equiv 9 \quad \bmod 10 \tag{1}$$
$$x \equiv 8 \quad \bmod 9 \tag{2}$$
$$x \equiv 7 \quad \bmod 8 \tag{3}$$

$$x \equiv 6 \quad \text{mod } 7 \qquad\qquad\qquad\qquad\qquad\qquad (4)$$
$$x \equiv 5 \quad \text{mod } 6 \qquad\qquad\qquad\qquad\qquad\qquad (5)$$
$$x \equiv 4 \quad \text{mod } 5 \qquad\qquad\qquad\qquad\qquad\qquad (6)$$
$$x \equiv 3 \quad \text{mod } 4 \qquad\qquad\qquad\qquad\qquad\qquad (7)$$
$$x \equiv 2 \quad \text{mod } 3 \qquad\qquad\qquad\qquad\qquad\qquad (8)$$
$$x \equiv 1 \quad \text{mod } 2 \qquad\qquad\qquad\qquad\qquad\qquad (9)$$

Adding 1 to equations 1 to 9, we get

$$x + 1 \equiv 0 \qquad \text{mod } 2 \qquad\qquad\qquad\qquad\qquad (10)$$
$$x + 1 \equiv 0 \qquad \text{mod } 3 \qquad\qquad\qquad\qquad\qquad (11)$$
$$x + 1 \equiv 0 \qquad \text{mod } 4 \qquad\qquad\qquad\qquad\qquad (12)$$
$$x + 1 \equiv 0 \qquad \text{mod } 5 \qquad\qquad\qquad\qquad\qquad (13)$$
$$x + 1 \equiv 0 \qquad \text{mod } 6 \qquad\qquad\qquad\qquad\qquad (14)$$
$$x + 1 \equiv 0 \qquad \text{mod } 7 \qquad\qquad\qquad\qquad\qquad (15)$$
$$x + 1 \equiv 0 \qquad \text{mod } 8 \qquad\qquad\qquad\qquad\qquad (16)$$
$$x + 1 \equiv 0 \qquad \text{mod } 9 \qquad\qquad\qquad\qquad\qquad (17)$$

Combining (10) through (17), we get

$$x + 1 \equiv 0 \qquad \text{mod LCM } (2, 3, 4, 5, 6, 7, 8, 9) \text{ or}$$
$$x + 1 \equiv 0 \qquad \text{mod } 2520$$

The smallest value for x is $2520 - 1 = 2519$.

2000 National Team Round Solutions

1. **Solution:** 50 (cubic centimeters).

The volume of the resulting cone is

$$V = \frac{1}{3}\pi r^2 h.$$

 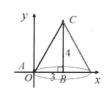 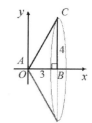

If the triangle is rotated around BC, the volume is

$$V_1 = \frac{1}{3}\pi r_1^2 h_1 = \frac{1}{3}\pi (3)^2 \times 4 = 12\pi \approx 38.$$

If the triangle is rotated around AB, the volume is

$$V_2 = \frac{1}{3}\pi r_2^2 h_2 = \frac{1}{3}\pi (4)^2 \times 3 = 16\pi \approx 50.$$

The greatest volume is 50.

2. **Solution:** 4/7.
Case 1:
Erica flips and does not win
Nate flips and wins

Probability: $1 \times \dfrac{1}{2} = (\dfrac{1}{2})^1$.

Case 2:
Erica flips and does not win
Nate flips and does not win
Noah flips and does not win
Erica flips and does not win
Nate flips and wins

Probability: $1 \times \dfrac{1}{2} \times \dfrac{1}{2} \times \dfrac{1}{2} \times \dfrac{1}{2} = (\dfrac{1}{2})^4$.

Case 3:

Erica flips and does not win
Nate flips and does not win
Noah flips and does not win
Erica flips and does not win
Nate flips and does not win
Noah flips and does not win
Erica flips and does not win
Nate flips and wins

Probability: $1 \times \dfrac{1}{2} \times \dfrac{1}{2} \times \dfrac{1}{2} \quad \times \dfrac{1}{2} \times \dfrac{1}{2} \times \dfrac{1}{2} \times \dfrac{1}{2} = (\dfrac{1}{2})^7$.

The pattern continues and we see it forms an infinite geometric series with first

term $a = \dfrac{1}{2}$ and common ratio $r = (\dfrac{1}{2})^3$.

The infinite geometric series sum is $\dfrac{a}{1-r} = \dfrac{\dfrac{1}{2}}{1-(\dfrac{1}{2})^3} = \dfrac{4}{7}$.

3. **Solution:** 180,001.
We group the numbers from 0 to 9999 into pairs: (0, 9999), (1, 9998), (3, 9997),… and remember to include the number 10,000 in our final calculation.

There are 5,000 pairs and in each pair, the sum of all the digits is $4 \times 9 = 36$. The sum of all the digits from 0 to 9999 is $36 \times 5000 = 180,000$.

The sum of the digits needed to write all the whole numbers from 0 to 10,000 inclusive equals $180,000 + 1(\text{for } 1000) = 180,001$.

4. **Solution:** 2.
Connect MN and AN. The radius of the circle is $AN = BN = BD/2 = 2$. From right triangle AMN, we get MN = $\sqrt{2}$.

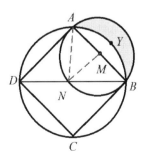

The quarter circle NAB has the area of $\dfrac{\pi \times (2)^2}{4} = \pi$.

The triangle NAB has the area of $\dfrac{AN \times BN}{2} = 2$.

The are of sector *AYB* is equal to the area of the area of the quarter circle *NAB* minus the area of the triangle *NAB*, or $\pi - 2$.

The shaded area is equal to the area of the area of the half circle *M* minus the area of the sector *AYB*, or

$$\frac{\pi \times (\sqrt{2})^2}{2} - (\pi - 2) = \pi - \pi + 2 = 2.$$

5. **Solution:** 11.25. (units).
Let *x* be half of the length of the fold.
EF is the perpendicular bisector of *AC*.

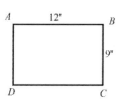

Since *AB* = 12 cm, *BC* = 9 cm, *AC* = 15 cm and *AE* = 15/2 cm, and $\triangle AEF \sim \triangle ABC$ (because two angles are the same),

$$\frac{AE}{AB} = \frac{EF}{BC}$$

$$\Rightarrow \quad \frac{\dfrac{15}{2}}{12} = \frac{x}{9}$$

$$\Rightarrow \quad x = \frac{\dfrac{15}{2}}{12} \times 9 = \frac{45}{8}.$$

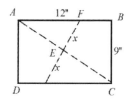

The length of the fold is $2x = 2x = 2 \times \dfrac{45}{8} = 11.25$.

6. **Solution:** $\dfrac{1}{24}$.

The probability of rolling an even number is $\dfrac{3}{6}$, and the probability of rolling the same even number again is $\dfrac{1}{6}$.

The probability of rolling an odd number is $\dfrac{3}{6}$ and the probability of rolling the

same odd number again is $\dfrac{1}{6}$.

There are $\dfrac{4!}{2!2!}$ ways to order EEOO.

The total probability is then $\dfrac{3}{6} \times \dfrac{1}{6} \times \dfrac{1}{6} \times \dfrac{3}{6} \times \dfrac{4!}{2!2!} = \dfrac{1}{24}$.

7. Solution: 2105352.
Let five positive integers be a, b, c, d, and e.

We have $a + b + c + d + e = 92$.

For the product to be the greatest, the numbers must be as close to each other as possible.

Since $95 \div 5 = 18.4$, each number should be as close as possible to 18, yielding $18 + 18 + 18 + 19 + 19 = 92$.
The greatest product is $18 \times 18 \times 18 \times 19 \times 19 = 2105352$.

8. Solution: $\dfrac{7}{45}$.
There are a total of $6 \times 6 \times 5$ numbers that can be formed using the digits 0, 1, 3, 6, 7, 8 and 9 such that no digit is repeated in any number.

In order to be divisible by 4, the last two digits of the number must be divisible by 4. The tens digit must also be greater than 2 such that the number is more than 300.

This gives us the following cases:
Last two digits
08	4 such numbers (308, 608, 708, 908).
16	4 such numbers (316, 716, 816, 916).
36	3 such numbers (736, 836, 936).
60	4 such numbers (360, 760, 860, 960).

68	3 such numbers (368, 768, 968).
76	3 such numbers (476, 876, 976).
80	4 such numbers (380, 680, 780, 980).
96	3 such numbers (396, 796, 896).

There are $4 + 4 + 3 + 4 + 3 + 3 + 4 + 3 = 28$ such numbers.

The probability is $\dfrac{28}{6 \times 6 \times 5} = \dfrac{7}{45}$.

9. **Solution:** 0.57.

The diameter of the largest circle is $2 \times 6 = 12$. Its area is 36π.

The side length of the largest square is $\dfrac{12}{\sqrt{2}} = 6\sqrt{2}$. Its area is 72.

It follows that the area of $4a$ is $36\pi - 72$.

The diameter of the second largest circle is $6\sqrt{2}$. Its area is 18π.
The side length of the second largest square is 6. Its area is 36.
It follows that the area of $4b$ is $18\pi - 36$.

Similarly, the diameter of the smallest circle is 6. Its area is 9π.

The side length of the smallest square is $\dfrac{6}{\sqrt{2}} = 3\sqrt{2}$. Its area is 18.

The area of $4c$ is $9\pi - 18$.

The shaded area is $4a + 4b + 4c = 36\pi - 72 + 18\pi - 36 + 9\pi - 18 = 63\pi - 126$.
The unshaded area is $36\pi - (63\pi - 126) = 126 - 27\pi$.

The ratio is $\dfrac{126 - 27\pi}{63\pi - 126} = 0.57$.

10. Solution: 14.
Let the sides of right triangle be x, y, and z as shown.
Method 1:

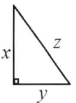

$$x^2 + y^2 = z^2 \qquad\qquad (1)$$
$$x^2 + y^2 + z^2 = 1352 \qquad\qquad (2)$$

Substituting (1) into (2), we get
$$2z^2 = 1352$$
$$\Rightarrow\ z^2 = 676$$
$$\Rightarrow\ z = 26.$$
A Pythagorean Triple where the hypotenuse is 26 is (10, 24, 26).

The perimeter is indeed 60. The positive difference between the lengths of the two legs is $24 - 10 = 14$.

Method 2:
$$x + y + z = 60 \qquad\qquad (1)$$
$$x^2 + y^2 = z^2 \qquad\qquad (2)$$
$$x^2 + y^2 + z^2 = 1352 \qquad\qquad (3)$$

Substituting (1) into (2):
$$2z^2 = 1352$$
$$\Rightarrow\ z^2 = 676$$
$$\Rightarrow\ z = 26.$$

Substituting 26 for z into (1) and (2), we get
$$x + y = 34 \qquad\qquad (4)$$
$$x^2 + y^2 = 676 \qquad\qquad (5)$$
Squaring both sides of (4):
$$x^2 + 2xy + y^2 = 1156$$
$$\Rightarrow\qquad 2xy = 480$$

$\Rightarrow \qquad -2xy = -480$ $\qquad\qquad\qquad$ (6)

Adding (5) + (6):

$x^2 - 2xy + y^2 = 196$

$\Rightarrow (x - y)^2 = 14^2$.

The positive difference between the lengths of the two legs is $|x - y| = 14$.

Notes:

(1) This attachment contains the team round problems re-assembled in a special way that you can practice them as target round problems. The problems are presented in pairs. The time limit for each pair of problems is six minutes.

(2) This round assumes the use of calculators, and calculations may also be done on scratch paper, but no other aids are allowed.

(3) The problems attached are for your reference only. To avoid possible copyright issues, Yongcheng Chen changed the *wording* of each problem but not the *substance*, of the problems. Please refer to Mathcounts.org for original test problems if you have any question.

(4) The book's original price is not changed by adding the attachment to the book.

1990 Mathcounts National Team Round Problems

1. Find the number of squares in the figure below.

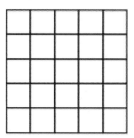

10. A sheet of rectangular paper with length $z + 2x$ and width $2y + 2x$ is cut and folded with no overlap to form a closed box with volume xyz. What is the total area, in terms of x and y, of the paper that is thrown away?

2. A credit union issues credit card numbers consisting of nine digits. The card number is designed so that its ninth (last) digit is the remainder obtained when the sum of the two-digit numbers formed by the four pairs of preceding digits is divided by a one-digit integer x. If 83 46 38 97 5 and 79 86 95 64 2 are valid numbers, find x.

9. The function $s = -16t^2 + v_0 t + s_0$ gives the height s at times t of a projectile fired vertically from initial height, s_0, and initial velocity, v_0. Find the number of seconds it will take for a projectile fired with initial velocity 128 feet per second from initial height 144 feet to attain the height 336 feet for the second time.

3. A non-standard die has the six faces labeled with the digits 3, 4, 5, 6, 8, and 10. If two such dice are rolled, find the probability that the two faces showing have numbers that could correspond to any two sides of a right triangle, given that all three sides of the triangle have integral lengths. Express your answer as a common fraction.

8. A math club sold 200 tickets for $1.00 each. Three prizes are awarded in the amounts of $10, $50, and $100. How much money, in cents, does the math club make per ticket?

4. What is the perimeter of the polygon given below?

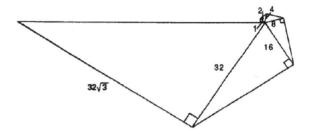

7. The counting numbers 1, 2, 3, ... are written consecutively. Find the 3001 st digit written.

5. In a game, Alex allows five points for each game he wins, seven points for each game his younger brother Bob wins, and three points for each game his younger sister Cathy wins. After a certain number of games, all three have identical scores. Find the fewest number of games they could have played in order for this tie to be possible.

6. Each of three figures represents objects on a balance scale. Express ⬤ in terms of ◯.

fig. 1

fig. 2

fig. 3

.

1991 Mathcounts National Team Round Problems

1. A cube of side 1 inch is cut from each corner of a cube of side 3 inches. A cube of side 2 inches is then inserted in each corner. Find the surface area of the resulting solid in square inches.

10. A tape can record 6 hours on extra–long play, 4 hours on long play, or 2 hours on short play. The tape has been used 32 minutes on short play and 44 minutes on long play. Find the number of minutes it still can record on extra–long play.

2. As shown in the figure, each side of the square is 6 cm. Four quarter circles are drawn with the centers at four vertices of the square. What is the area in square centimeters of the shaded region if the radius of each circle is $2\sqrt{3}$ cm? Express your answer in simplest radical form in terms of π.

9. Find the area of the shaded region in the figure below. Round your answer to the nearest square centimeter.

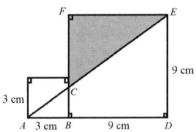

70

3. Now the time is between 4:00 and 5:00. What time will the hour hand and the minute hand form exactly 10° angle the first time?

8. The first three hexagonal numbers are 1, 6, and 15 as represented in the figure shown. What is the sum of the first five hexagonal numbers?

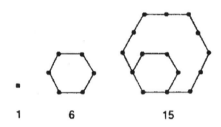

1   6   15

4. A bubble of spherical shape lands on a horizontal surface and forms a hemisphere of the same volume. What is the radius of the original bubble if the radius of the hemisphere is $3\sqrt[3]{2}$ cm?

7. A math class of 20 students are randomly paired to take a test. Find the probability that Curtis and Cameron, two students in the class, are paired with each other. Express your answer as a common fraction.

5. A test consists of 100 true – false questions. Every question that is a multiple of 4 is true. And all others are false. A student marks every item that is a multiple of 3 false and all others true. Find the number of questions that will be correctly answered.

6. A sheet of rectangular paper with length 12 inches and width 9 inches is folded such that one corner is onto the diagonally opposite corner. Find the length in inches of the crease. Express your answer as a mixed number.

1992 Mathcounts National Team Problems

1. Find the number of times the digit "4" appears in the integer part of the quotient $10^{100} \div 7$.

10. We find the digital root of a number by adding the digits of the number, adding the digits of the resulting number, and so on, until the result is a single digit. If we randomly select an integer n from 1 through 10, find the probability that the digital root of n^3 equals 1. Express your answer as a common fraction.

2. Find the last two digits of 2^{222}.

9. Find the number of cards that must be selected from a standard deck to be certain that three cards from the same suit are drawn.

3. What is the smallest (positive) integer n for which: $\dfrac{1}{1^2} + \dfrac{1}{2^2} + \ldots + \dfrac{1}{n^2} > \dfrac{3}{2}$?

8. What is the area of the region determined by the system of inequalities:

$y \geq |x|$

$y \leq -|x+1| + 4$?

Express your answer as a decimal.

4. Every circle in the figure shown has a radius of 6 cm. What is the area, in square centimeters, of the shaded region? Round your answer to the nearest square centimeter. Use 3.14 for π.

7. In the figure, the square has the side length of 100 cm. Point *A* is the center of the square. The shaded region has an area that is one-fifth of the area of the square. Find *x*, in centimeters.

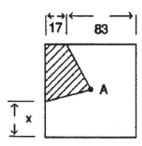

5. A circle of radius 4 is inscribed in a triangle. One side of the triangle is divided into segments of lengths 6 cm and 8 cm by the point of tangency. Find the length, in centimeters, of the shortest side of the triangle.

6. The pages of a book are numbered using 510 digits with the first page of the book is numbered "1". Find the number of pages of the book.

.

1993 Mathcounts National Team Round Problems
1. What is the sum of the digits in the decimal representation of $(789,000,003,450,000)^2$?

10. Given that $(a + b):(b + c):(c + a)=6 : 7: 8$ and $a + b + c = 14$, what is the value of c?

2. The sum of two numbers is 12 and the product is −4. What is the sum of their reciprocals?

9. At most 3 faces can be seen from one direction when observing a die. Find the number that cannot be the sum of the observed faces from the following numbers: 5, 6, 7, 8, 9, 10, 11, 12, 13, 14, 15.

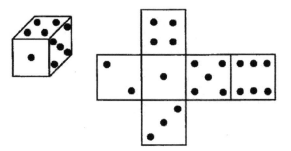

3. In the multiplication shown, each letter represents a different digit. Find the largest possible value of D. A is not zero.

$$\begin{array}{r} ABC \\ \times \quad C \\ \hline DBC \end{array}$$

8. What is the sum $\dfrac{1}{1\times 3}+\dfrac{1}{3\times 5}+\dfrac{1}{5\times 7}+\dfrac{1}{(7\times 9)}+...+\dfrac{1}{199\times 201}$?

4. The teacher whispers positive integer A to Anna, B to Brett, and C to Chris. The students don't know one another's numbers but they do know that the sum of their numbers is 14. Anna says: "I know that Brett and Chris have different numbers." Then Brett says: "I already knew that all three of our numbers were different." Finally, Chris announces: "Now I know all three of our numbers." Find the product ABC.

7. A frustum of a right circular cone is used as a water container. The top base of the frustum has a radius one-half that of the bottom base. If a mark halfway up the side says "200 gallons," how many gallons of water, to the nearest tenth, can the frustum hold?

5. The 5 letters of the word COUNT can be permutated to produce 5! = 120 different strings of 5 letters. If these strings are put in alphabetical order, in which position will the string TNUOC fall?

6. Points A and D are the centers of two circles of radius 10 inches each as shown in the figure. If $AD = 10$ inches, find the area of the shaded region of square $ABCD$. Express your answer in square inches to the nearest hundredth.

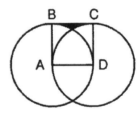

.

1994 Mathcounts National Team Round Problems

1. If $\boxed{a\ b} = ab - a - b$, what is the integer value of x such that $= 31$.

10. The edge of the base of a square pyramid is six inches and the height is six inches as well. The volume of a square pyramid is then cut by a plane parallel to the base into two equal amounts. What is the distance from the plane to the base of the pyramid? Express your answer in simplest radical form.

2. As shown in the figure, four squares have a common vertex. $AB = \frac{2}{3} AC$, $AC = \frac{2}{3} AD$, and $AD = \frac{2}{3} AE$. Find the reduced ratio of the smaller shaded area to the larger shaded area. Express your answer as a common fraction.

9. Find the value of n if $3^{1993} = 100k + n$. n is a nonnegative integer less than 100.

3. As shown in the figure, a triangle is inscribed in a square of the side length of 2". Find the length of a side of the triangle if it is equilateral. Express your answer in decimal form to the nearest hundredth of an inch.

.

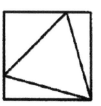

8. As shown in the figure, AB is a straight line with $AB = 2AC = 3AE = 4DB$. If a point x is randomly selected on AB, find the probability that x is between E and C. Express your answer as a common fraction.

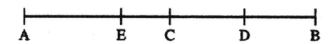

4. There are 225 steps from the subway stop to street level. Susan can climb stairs at a rate of 45 steps per minute. The escalator travels at a rate of 75 steps per minute. Find the number of minutes that Susan will use to climb up the moving escalator. Express your answer as a mixed number.

7. Ten standard dice are rolled and the product of the top faces is $2^5 \cdot 3^5$. Find the largest possible sum of these faces.

5. Select four different digits at random from the digits 1 through 9 to form all possible four-digit numbers. The sum of these numbers is S. F is the greatest common factor of all such sums. What is the value of F?

6. A solid figure is obtained by rotating the segment of $2x + 3y = 6$ in the first quadrant around the x-axis. Find the ratio of the surface area to the volume of this solid. Express your answer as a common fraction in simplest radical form.

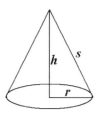

1995 Mathcounts National Team Round Problems

1. A dart is thrown randomly at the dart board shown. The radius of the large circle is 10. Find the probability that it will land inside the square but not inside the inner circle. Express your answer rounded to the nearest whole percent.

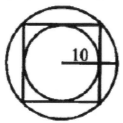

10. The counting numbers from 1 to 1,000 are listed consecutively in a triangle as shown. Each row contains one more number than the row below. Find the number directly above 723.

```
...
11    12    13    14    15
7     8     8     10
4     5     6
2     3
1
```

2. Five points are placed in different ways in a plane so that two or more of them are collinear. A set is formed consisting of the total numbers of distinct lines that can be drawn to pass through any two or more points in each of the possible 5-point configurations. Find the median of this set.

9. Sally is 24 years of age and is twice as old as Allie was when Sally was as old as Allie is now. How many years old is Allie now?

3. A binomial has the form $ma + nb$, where m and n are natural numbers. If there are three such binomials and their sum is $4a + 8b$, how many distinct sets of such three binomials exist?

8. Alex cut $2\dfrac{1}{2}$ ″ diameter cookies from dough rolled into a $10'' \times 18\dfrac{1}{2}$ ″ rectangle as shown below. After cutting, he rolls the remaining dough into a rectangle of the same thickness. Find the greatest number of whole cookies that he can cut out on the next rolling.

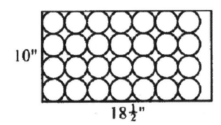

4. The wheels of a car turn 400 times a minute. The diameters of each wheel is three feet. Find the number of miles per hour the car is traveling. Express your answer rounded to the nearest whole number.

7. Star polygons can be generated as follows: n points are equally distributed around the circumference of a unit circle. An initial point P_0 is chosen and each of the remaining points are then consecutively labeled clockwise P_1, P_2, ..., P_{n-1}. Segment P_0P_m is constructed where $0 < m < n$; then a chord of the same length is constructed beginning at P_m and ending at the mth point counting clockwise from P_m. This procedure is repeated until arriving at P_0. The figure is a star polygon only if all n points were used to construct the segments. Find the number of distinct star polygons if $n = 36$.

5. Jane is building a ladder with 9 equally spaced rungs between two straight sides. The lowest rung (rung 1) is 24 inches wide and the uppermost rung is 18 inches wide. What is the sum of the lengths of rungs 4 and 5? Express your answer as a decimal to the nearest hundredth

6. Find the number of even integers between 8,000 and 9,999 having digits that are all distinct.

1996 Mathcounts National Team Round Problems

1. A box of cereal is charged a fixed rate per ounce of cereal and a fixed price for the empty box, regardless of its size. If a box containing 12 ounces of cereal costs $3.35 and a box with 18 ounces of cereal costs $4.67, find the number of cents in the fixed price of the empty box.

10. As shown in the figure, for $\angle A$ of triangle ABC to be the largest angle, it must be that $m < x < n$. Find the greatest possible value of $n - m$. Express the answer as a common fraction.

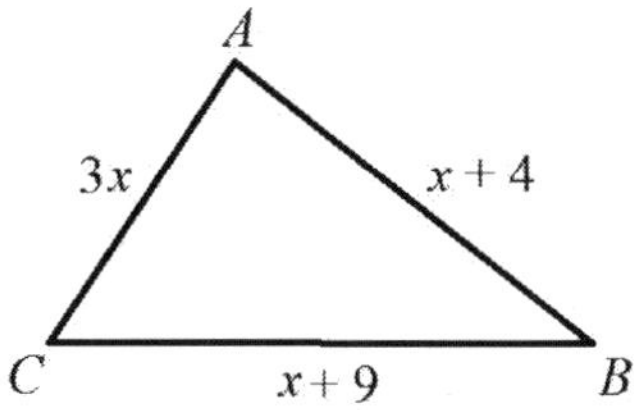

2. What is the sum of the three smallest positive solutions to $x - [x] = \dfrac{1}{[x]}$? $[x]$ is called the greatest integer function, denotes the largest integer less than or equal to x. For example, $[3.5] = 3$, $[\pi] = 3$ and $[-\pi] = -4$. Express your answer as a mixed number.

9. What is the product of the four smallest positive integers with an even number of distinct factors?

3. All points with coordinates (m, n) form the set S. m and n are integers, $0 \leq m \leq 4$ and $0 \leq n \leq 4$. If two points from S are randomly chosen, find is the probability that the midpoint of the segment joining the two points is also in S. Express your answer as a common fraction.

8. The first ten rows of an auditorium each contain 20 seats. After the tenth row, each row has 2 more seats than the previous row. Find the number of seats in the auditorium if the auditorium has 80 rows of seats.

4. A seven-element data lists of integers in numerical order to fit the following criteria: the mean is 20; the median is 21; the mode is 22 and unique; and the range is 10. Find the number of ways to write such seven-element data lists.

7. Emma randomly selected a diagonal of a regular octagon. Tina randomly selected one of the remaining diagonals. What is the probability that the diagonals they selected have the same length? Express your answer as a common fraction.

5. As shown in the figure, each region represents $\frac{1}{12}$ of the total area. What is the ratio of the radius of the innermost of the three concentric circles to the radius of the outer circle? Express your answer as a decimal to the nearest hundredth.

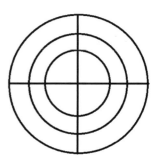

6. What is the three-digit number n with three distinct digits which has one digit in the same place and one digit in a different place as each of 836, 315 and 983?

1997 Mathcounts National Team Round Problems

1. There are three different positive integers. Their sum is less than 20 and their product is 144. The difference between the greatest integer and the least integer is 5. Find the greatest of these three integers.

10. Find the number of triangles that can be formed whose vertices are dots in the 3 × 7 rectangular array as shown.

```
•  •  •  •  •  •  •
•  •  •  •  •  •  •
•  •  •  •  •  •  •
```

2. With each change, the central one-fourth of every white equilateral triangle is shaded. Find the fractional part of the original equilateral triangle that would be shaded after four changes. Express your answer as a common fraction.

9. As shown in the figure, two semicircles are inscribed in a rectangle so their diameters are opposite sides of the rectangle. Find the probability that a point randomly selected inside the rectangle will also be inside both semicircles. Express your answer as a decimal rounded to the nearest hundredth.

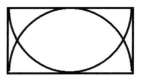

3. When a positive integer is divided by 5, the remainder is 4; when divided by 6, the remainder is 5; when divided by 7, the remainder is 6; when divided by 8, the remainder is 7; when divided by 9, the remainder is 8; and when divided by 10, the remainder is 9. Find the least value of the positive integer.

8. A square pyramid has a base edge of 6 cm and an altitude of 10 cm. A cut is made parallel to the base of the pyramid that separates it into a smaller pyramid and a frustum. If each base edge of the smaller pyramid is 3 cm, find the total surface area of the frustum. Express your answer rounded to the nearest whole square cm.

4. Using the figure shown to find the radius of the circle which passes through points X, Y and Z. Express your answer as a decimal rounded to the nearest tenth.

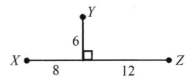

7. Find the number of positive three-digit integers less than 400 satisfy each of the following characteristics simultaneously:
A. Each of the three digits is prime.
B. The sum of the three digits is prime.
C. The number is prime.

5. Find the number of positive three-digit integers for which the tens digit exceeds the sum of the other two digits.

6. The vertices of a rectangle are A(0, 0), B(5,0), C(5,3) and D(0,3). The rectangular region determined by these points is rotated 360° about the y − axis, forming a solid. The rectangular region is then rotated 360° about the x − axis, forming another solid. Find the number of cubic units in the positive difference between the volumes of these two solids. Express your answer in terms of π.

1998 Mathcounts National Team Round Problems

1. In a math club, $66\frac{2}{3}\%$ of the girls and $71\frac{3}{7}\%$ of the boys wear watches. The same number of boys and girls wear watches. If five girls do not wear watches, Find the number of students in the club.

10. A floor in rectangle shape is covered with square tiles. The floor is 81 tiles long and 63 tiles wide. If a diagonal is drawn across the floor, find the number of tiles the diagonal will cross?

2. Two equilateral triangles $\triangle ABC$ and $\triangle PQR$ are shown in the figure. AQ, RC and BP are congruent and bisect their respective angles. The four interior regions $AQPB$, $AQRC$, $BPRC$ and QPR all have the same area. If $AB = 20$ cm, find the number of centimeters in PB. Express your answer as a decimal to the nearest hundredth.

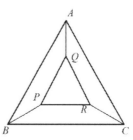

9. Find the smallest positive integer that cannot be expressed as the sum of eight or fewer cubes of positive integers.

3. The equation $37x + 73y = 2016$ is satisfied by exactly one ordered pair of positive integers (x, y). Find the sum $x + y$.

8. Find the least two–digit integer whose cube has the same tens and units digits as the integer.

4. A round table touches two walls as shown in the figure. Point *A* is on the outer edge of the table and is 2 inches from one of the walls. If the radius of the table is 37 inches, find the distance of point *A* to the other wall.

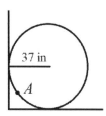

7. An ant located at corner A likes to travel to corner B of a 4" × 6" × 8" rectangular box. The ant can only travel on the faces of the box. Find the least number of inches that the ant must travel. Express your answer as a decimal to the nearest hundredth.

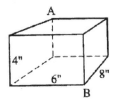

5. Bob and Bill had a 24-kilometer race. Bob's speed was 12 kilometers per hour for the first half distance and 8 kilometers per hour for the other half.
Bill ran half the time at 12 kilometers per hour and the other half at 8 kilometers per hour. By how many minutes did Bill win the race?

6. There are 6 red marbles and 4 blue marbles in a mayonnaise jar. There are 2 red marbles and 5 blue marbles in a jelly jar. One marble is randomly selected from the mayonnaise jar and placed in the jelly jar. A marble is then randomly selected from the jelly jar. Find the probability that the selected marble is red. Express your answer as a common fraction.

1999 Mathcounts National Team Round Problems

1. Find the number of different paths go from *A* to *Z* using only the paths that follow the line segments and go downward.

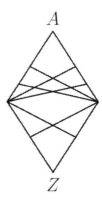

10. Find the smallest whole number such that, when divided by each of 10, 9, 8, 7, ... , 2, gives a remainder of 9, 8, 7, 6, ... ,1, respectively.

2. A circular window is divided into nine regions of the same area as shown. The inner circular pane has a diameter of 8 inches. Find the number of inches in the distance from A to B. Express your answer as a decimal to the nearest tenth.

9. As shown below, a square can be partitioned into four smaller squares, or nine smaller squares, or even into seven smaller squares provided the squares don't have to be congruent. (Note that overlapping squares are not counted twice.) Find the greatest integer n such that a square cannot be partitioned into n smaller squares.

3. Find the value of $\dfrac{1}{x^2} + \dfrac{1}{y^2}$ if $x - y = -10$ and $xy = 20$. Express your answer as a common fraction.

8. The height is 12 feet and the circumference is 2 feet of a cylindrical pole. A rope is attached to a point on the circumference at the bottom of the pole. The rope is then wrapped tightly around the pole four times before it reaches a point on the top directly above the starting point at the bottom. Find the minimum number of feet in the length of the rope. Express your answer in simplest radical form.

4. A triangle has the side lengths of 6 cm, 50 cm and 52 cm. Find the number of centimeters in the length of the altitude to the shortest side of the triangle.

7. *ABFE* and *MNRQ* are two rectangular pieces of paper, measuring $1'' \times 2''$ and $1'' \times 3''$, respectively. Each is folded such that one corner is onto the diagonally opposite corner along *EF* and *QR*, respectively (Points *B* and *D* coincide and points *N* and *P* coincide). Find the ratio of the area of *ABFE* to the area of *MNRQ*. Express your answer as a common fraction.

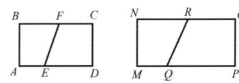

5. As shown in the figure, a regular hexagon is inscribed in a circle of radius 3 in. Six arcs are then drawn with a vertex as the center and the side length of the hexagon as the radius. Find the area of the shaded region in square inches. Express your answer as a decimal to the nearest hundredth.

6. Find the smallest possible value for $x + y$ if $\dfrac{1}{x} + \dfrac{1}{y} = \dfrac{1}{12}$. Both x and y are positive integers and $x \neq y$.

2000 Mathcounts National Team Round Problems

1. *ABC* is a right triangle with legs *AB* = 3cm and *CB* = 4 cm. When *ABC* is rotated about one of its legs, find the greatest possible number of cubic centimeters in the volume of the resulting solid. Express your answer to the nearest whole number.

10. A right triangle has the perimeter 60 inches. The sum of the squares of lengths of three sides is 1352. Find the number of inches in the positive difference between the lengths of the two legs.

2. Three students (Erica, Nate, and Noah) are playing a game by flipping a fair coin in turns. Erica flips the coin first. Nate then flips the coin and wins if it matches Erica's flip. If it doesn't match, then Noah flips the coin and wins if it matches Nate's flip. If Noah doesn't win, then Erica flips and wins if it matches Noah's flip. The game continues until there is a winner. Find the probability that Nate wins the game. Express your answer as a common fraction.

9. The largest circle shown has the radius of 6 cm. Find the ratio of the area of the unshaded region to the area of the shaded region. Express your answer as a decimal to the nearest hundredth.

3. Find the sum of the digits needed to write all the whole numbers from 0 to 10,000, inclusive.

8. Use the digits 0, 1, 3, 6, 7, 8 and 9 to form all possible three-digit positive integers with no digit repeated in any number. Then select one of these numbers at random. Find the probability that it will be greater than 300 and divisible by 4. Express your answer as a common fraction.

4. Two circles M and N intersect at A and B. Find the area of the shaded region in square centimeters if $ABCD$ is a square with $BD = 4$ cm.

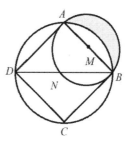

7. The sum of five positive integers is 92. Find the greatest possible product.

5. A sheet of rectangular paper $ABCD$ with length 12 inches and width 9 inches is folded such that that A and C coincide. Find the number of inches in the length of the fold. Express your answer as a decimal to the nearest hundredth.

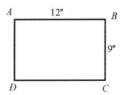

6. Four standard dice are rolled. Find the probability that two of the numbers are the same even number and that the other two numbers are the same odd number. Express your answer as a common fraction.

Made in the USA
Lexington, KY
02 May 2018